HOW TO DECODE ESSAY TITLES

MAKING SENSE OF ESSAY QUESTIONS AT UNIVERSITY

How To Decode Essay Titles: Making Sense of Essay Questions at University
Copyright © 2014 John Richard Henderson

ISBN-13: 978-1496180438
ISBN-10: 1-496-18043-7

Structural Editor: Sarah Barbour
Copy Editor: RJ Locksley

Published: July 2014 by Books That Explain
www.BooksThatExplain.com

Printed by CreateSpace

All rights reserved. No part of this publication may be reprinted or reproduced, stored in retrieval system, copied in any form or by any means, electronic, mechanical, photocopying, recording or otherwise transmitted without written permission from the publisher. You must not circulate this book in any format.

CONTENTS

1. The student's predicament   1

2. Solving the problem   7

3. Tasks that lead to an outline   17

4. Tasks that don't lead to an outline   29

5. Developing the subject   43

6. Finding sources of information   57

7. Concluding the whole process   67

8. Worked Examples   73

9. Author's note   95

CHAPTER 1
THE STUDENT'S PREDICAMENT

Imagine the scene...

You're sitting at your desk and you have an essay to write. Naturally, you want to produce the best piece of work that you can because there are rewards for doing so: a good grade, praise from your lecturer, a better understanding of your subject and a feeling of pride and accomplishment.

So where do you start? Well, everyone knows that a good essay must answer the question that's been given. But as you scan over the list of titles set by your lecturer, you discover that rather than being helpful and explanatory, each one is an abrupt little package of obscure words and cryptic demands:

>'Assess the relevance...'
>'Explore the theory...'
>'Critically examine...'
>'Evaluate.'
>'Discuss.'

Argh! What do any of these mean? What are they asking you to do? And if you're not sure, how are you supposed to write that fabulous essay? This is serious. If you don't understand the question, you've lost the race at the very first hurdle.

A deadline is looming and you don't even know what you're expected to do.

The situation seems hopeless.

The rules have changed—but nobody told you!

Things were so much simpler at school.

Back then, essay questions were easy to understand and always echoed the ideas that had been discussed in class. Usually, a single textbook was chosen and supplied by the teacher, so nobody needed to hunt around the library. Nor did anyone need to wonder what information they had to find because that was, again, specified by the teacher.

At school, you could take comfort from knowing what you had to do to get a good grade. When marking papers, the teacher would be checking that children had absorbed what he or she had taught. So when an essay conformed to the classroom material, a high mark would be awarded. Once you'd figured out how the system worked, you could simply churn out what your teacher expected to see, and earn yourself an 'A'.

But once you get to university, you suddenly find that the rules have changed. Instead of supplying everything that an undergraduate needs, *these* teachers expect students to be much more self-reliant. Let's see what that means in practice…

The purpose of writing essays

School and university have differing views on what an essay is supposed to deliver. As I mentioned above, school simply asked you to demonstrate that you had learned the material taught in class. But on a university's arts and humanities courses, the focus shifts from correct answers to correct methods. Lecturers are not assessing *what students know*, but rather *how students think*, and this leads to essay questions that are much more involved than those you were given at school.

Moreover, questions in the arts and humanities often have no 'correct' answer—so you aren't expected to supply one. Instead, students must construct *their own* individual and well-reasoned answer to such a question.

How do you deliver this?

When students are asked to provide their own unique response, that doesn't mean it's okay to simply offer a scrapbook of interesting facts relating to the title. Nor should anyone just blast out an opinionated monologue. Instead, you must convince your lecturer that you have a valid viewpoint by building a persuasive case or 'argument' which lays out the thought process that leads to your final conclusions. Assignment questions at college often expect students to weigh up evidence and arrive at a decisive judgement—just like an official inquiry or a judicial ruling.

It's worth noting at this point that two people can each hand in an essay with wildly differing opinions, but both be awarded high marks *if* they have both done a good job of constructing a credible case to support their conclusions.

The subject of the essay question

Unlike school, the subject of an essay question at university won't always be limited to the ideas that have already been discussed in class. This explains why some titles seem so mystifying or downright scary: students might have only been given *part* of the picture.

At university, your lectures won't supply all of the information that you need to know. Yes, really! Instead, undergraduates are expected to 'read around' their subject and independently expand their own knowledge. A full understanding of an essay title might only be possible when you have picked up some books and taught yourself some new stuff.

Using information

I mentioned 'weighing up evidence' just a minute ago. Where does this evidence come from? The case that you're trying to build will gain credibility by citing facts and ideas found in books and journals. University lecturers will expect an essay to reach out to your course's existing literature, by referring

The student's predicament

to it, quoting from it, questioning it and using it to either support or challenge your essay's argument.

If a lecturer supplies a reading list, it's up to you to assess which books are relevant to a particular assignment, to discover any additional books which are relevant but which *aren't* on the list, and finally, to acquire and read those books.

Back in the school classroom, textbooks tended to be looked upon as The Truth. However, while researching at undergraduate level, you will find that sources of information often conflict with each other; Book 'A' will declare one thing, while Book 'B' will completely disagree. This is where you get the chance to show off the types of thinking that deal with such inconsistencies:

- *Analytical thinking:* getting a deeper understanding of some evidence by pulling it apart to examine why it's significant or how it connects to other things. In other words, 'What does this tell me? What can I reasonably infer from this? How does it fit into the big picture?'
- *Critical thinking:* assessing the merits and faults of an argument or a piece of evidence and evaluating its reliability. In other words, 'How accurate is this material? Does it agree with other evidence? How much can I rely upon it?'

These can be applied to original material (e.g. historical documents, raw statistics or a playwright's manuscript, which are known as 'primary sources') and also to other writers' ideas about that original material (e.g. textbooks, journal articles and critical essays, otherwise known as 'secondary sources').

When employing evidence to support your argument, the assignment shouldn't only be a one-sided sales pitch. Students exhibit good 'academic style' by balancing their own opinions with other people's arguments and honestly showing how alternative views test the weak spots in their own position.

Are there any other academic conventions?

After entering academia, students are expected to present their work as a meaningful piece of research that abides by the conventions of academic writing.

For example, your work will talk and use vocabulary at a level which assumes that its readers have a particular degree of understanding. You *could* write in a way that would be comprehensible to the man on the street, but that would mean starting at a very elementary level and explaining a lot of terms. Instead, you should assume that your audience is at about the same level of understanding as yourself: perhaps an undergraduate on a course similar to your own.

Your work will also need to mimic that measured and dispassionate tone of voice that you can detect when you read existing academic research. Finally, you'll want to provide a properly formatted list of academic references at the end of the assignment that cites all of the sources to which you've referred.

Chapter summary

- You're supposed to work out what kind of essay you're expected to write by reading the question. But very often, essay questions are so perplexing that you can't make any sense of them.
- Your school experience doesn't help you here because now that you're at university, the rules of the game have changed.
- You're accustomed to showing your teachers what you've learned—but now they want to see how you think.
- So the questions have become more demanding and they might not even have a correct answer.
- Your lectures won't tell you everything you need to know and the books that you must consult often disagree with one another.
- Your essay should display analytical and critical thinking, a viewpoint that's balanced with other opinions, the specialist vocabulary of your academic discipline and a measured and objective tone of voice.

Argument: A persuasive case or process of reasoning.

Primary source: Original material such as raw data, historical documentation or an unabridged manuscript.

Secondary source: Another writer's views and judgement of the original material.

CHAPTER 2
SOLVING THE PROBLEM

What you need to know from a question

As you've just seen, composing an essay at undergraduate level means that you have several conventions to abide by, a few obstacles to avoid and many decisions to make—and yet only **one** question from which to work.

It's vital that you squeeze as much information as possible from the title to guide the job of answering it. The clearer your understanding of what the question is demanding, the easier it will be for you to supply it. But if your grasp of the question is poor, you'll struggle to chart the way forward. In fact, lecturers sometimes accuse students of writing essays which wander from the question, so with the help of accurate information, this can be avoided.

So let's be more specific and make a wish list. What information would you really like to get out of an assignment title?

1. The task that you're being asked to perform and an idea of how you're supposed to do it

It's incredibly important that you know what an essay title wants you to do. And yet the 'command words' that you encounter—'explore', 'discuss', 'evaluate', 'assess'—do a poor job of defining exactly what you're supposed to deliver. So the first thing you need to know is:

What are you supposed to do?

And that will help to answer the question that naturally follows:

How are you supposed to do it?

2. A rough outline that will give you an idea of the essay's general structure

It's much easier to assemble a jigsaw when you have the picture on the box to guide you. Likewise, it's much easier to write an essay when you have a plan for its layout or 'mini-outline' to work from, like this roughly sketched example:

- Introduction, describing what this essay will be about
- Second section, which gives a brief history of the situation to be discussed
- Third section, which investigates the situation's most important factors
- Fourth section, which compares and assesses these factors
- Conclusion, which summarises and gives the author's viewpoint

A mini-outline will give you a clear picture of how many sections the essay will have, what the job of each section would be and how they connect to each other. But it will also indicate how well a prospective essay answers the question, allow you to visualise the possible arguments that you could construct and provide an idea of how information sources might be used within your work. So the second thing that you need to know from a question is very helpful indeed:

What should the end result roughly look like?

3. The subject area that you're supposed to focus upon, together with some way to expand upon that subject

Identifying a question's subject should be a straightforward job, as most are succinct and quite easy to spot; for example, 'the Napoleonic wars', 'the impact of mass media on society' or 'the activity of enzymes in the cell.' But while such brevity is ideal for precisely summing up a question's subject, it becomes a real drawback when you're trying to spin out a three-thousand-word assignment from such a short prompt. So if identifying a question's subject is relatively easy, the next thing to work out is how to expand upon it. In other words:

What is the question's subject and how can you get the most out of it?

4. The information sources that you'll need to find, read, record and refer to

When composing an essay, part of a student's work involves referring to the existing ideas of other writers. But of course, students need to restrict their attention to sources that are relevant. Otherwise, time will be wasted on reading and noting down information that doesn't benefit the end result. So, the fourth and final thing that you really need to know is:

How do you accurately identify the kind of information that will help your understanding and strengthen your assignment?

And that completes our wish list of things to gather from a title, which we can summarise as:

- Task
- Outline
- Subject
- Information sources

In essence, the resolution of these four items **is** the destination that you're trying to reach when decoding an essay title. The rest of this book is dedicated to satisfying these four requirements, and so when I need to, I'll refer back to them as Task-Outline-Subject-Information or TOSI.

The usual method for decoding a question

When you're trying to make sense of what an essay title is asking of you, the usual advice given by study skills books and webpages is: 'Identify the most important key words and underline them.' Although this might sound like a reasonable approach, I can see three glaring problems with it.

Firstly, this advice assumes that you already have the ability to accurately pinpoint the most critical words in a title. But if that were true, you wouldn't need to be on a college course to learn this stuff. So not knowing any better, students tend to underline every word that isn't 'the' or 'and'.

Secondly, this method assumes that a question contains so many words that underlining is necessary to make the most important ones stand out. But some titles are short, and this means that there isn't much to underline—or rather, there isn't much *not* to underline:

- What are the politics of place in *Mansfield Park*? (9 words)
- Assess the role of colour in packaging. (7 words)
- How revolutionary was the American Revolution? (6 words)

But even assuming that undergraduates are expert keyword-spotters and that every question contains a great number of words, the third and final problem is far more serious: What do you do next? Once you've identified and underlined all of the keywords, exactly what are you supposed to do with them? Let's remember that you're looking for guidance on the task that you're supposed to perform, the way your assignment might be structured, the subject that you're supposed to focus upon and the sources you should be researching. So how do a bunch of underlined words provide any of that guidance?

The nearest that anyone can get to an answer comes from a keyword table whose total assistance often amounts to lines like, "When a question includes the word 'discuss', you're being asked to discuss something."

Hmmm, right...

An alternative method

If you can't count on underlined keywords to help decode an essay title, what's the alternative?

Perhaps the solution is not to jump in and highlight particular words, but to step back and consider the purpose of the entire question: "What is this title asking me to do? What kind of task does it involve?" After looking at many titles in this way, a pattern begins to emerge which shows that questions can be separated into distinct groups based on the task that they are asking you to complete, rather than by scrutinising individual words.

For example, students will often find essay questions that ask them to compare two things, questions that ask them to contrast two things and questions that ask them to compare and contrast two things. Although the particular command words are different, the tasks that they're asking someone to complete are broadly similar. This means that the strategies for tackling them share a lot of common ground. Any information that helps to answer *one* of those questions is going to be helpful for *all* of them.

So here's the way forward: **by sorting all of the kinds of questions that students are likely to meet into a limited number of task types, it becomes possible to identify an individual title's task by simply comparing it with every category and looking for a match.**

And if each category also includes an explanation of what that task type is asking students to do and how a student should respond, you'll be able to establish the first of the TOSI items that you need to know from an essay question:

The task you're supposed to perform (and how).

Pinpointing a question's task type will reveal the job that it is asking you to do. But knowing this also improves the chances of shrewdly anticipating the kind of essay structure that will deliver what the title wants, which is the second item on the TOSI list:

The best way to outline the essay.

What about a title's subject? In many cases, it's easy to spot the subject upon which a question is centred. But that doesn't prevent students from running into a couple of problems:

- A question's subject area is usually very concisely defined. But such brevity is difficult to expand into a full-blown discussion that's thousands of words long.
- It's easy for students to overlook hints that are deliberately hidden within the question and intended to push the assignment in a particular direction.

Therefore, students need the techniques that can expand a succinctly described subject into a broad discussion, and they need the insight to spot any signals that direct them to answer the question in a particular way. These techniques and insights will give a more complete grasp of item three on the TOSI list:

What the subject is.

There comes a time when a student has to leave their desk to go and search for some books. *Groan!* However, if you have an understanding of the question's task, a feel for the kind of structure that the essay will adopt and some ideas on how to develop the question's subject, then the research stage becomes less of a speculative wander around the library—"Oh, this book looks like it might somehow be connected to my assignment title"—and much more of a targeted mission, digging up the material which will be helpful and useable. Armed with a wish list of questions that research sources need to answer, you can immediately filter out any texts which do not provide the information that you require. This would fulfil the fourth TOSI item:

What information to research.

———

These ideas form the basis of an alternative way to decode an essay title—one which really *does* deliver the guidance that students need. This method splits an essay question into two components—its task and its subject—and then uses them to establish a suitable outline and a list of specific goals that research activities must fulfil. The procedure can be split into three stages:

1. Classifying the task and establishing a suitable outline
- You'll compare your essay question to the examples given for seven different task types.
- When you find a match, you'll be given information which explains what that task type is asking you to do and also offers suggestions on how to respond.
- You'll apply the information and suggestions to your particular title, and perhaps make notes on the improved understanding that this gives you.

2. Developing the subject
- You'll pinpoint the question's subject and then identify the angles or aspects from which it can be viewed. This helps when planning the outline of the assignment.
- You'll also try to detect any clues within the question that are there to influence the way you answer it.
- Gathering together everything that has emerged from analysing the task and the subject, you should be able to sketch out a rough structure for your assignment—or at least confidently plot some of the points through which it should travel.

3. Finding sources of information
- At this stage, you'll have *some* insight into the way that your essay will respond to the title. But you'll also be able to recognise where the gaps in your knowledge are. This means that you will be able to assemble a list of specific questions that you need answers to.
- After conducting preliminary reading, you'll be able to note down the answers to (hopefully!) all of your questions and this should tidy up any remaining loose ends. You will also have gathered a list of the books and articles that you need to read for your in-depth research.

- Finally, you can sketch out a plan for your in-depth research and note-taking activities, and by now, you will also be able to visualise a number of ways in which you could answer the title. This means that you'll set out with purpose and confidence, rather than being overwhelmed by the quantity of available information.

Completing this three-stage process should endow you with a sheet of paper which tells you the job that the assignment is supposed to do, what subject area it will be talking about and a rough idea of its structure. This will then provide some leads to follow in the library and some clues for plotting the course of the essay.

So let's begin...

Chapter summary

- You're expected to compose a complex written piece of two or three thousand words with only a short, cryptic title to guide you.
- Ideally, there are four things that you need to establish from an essay question: its *task*, a suitable *outline* for your response, its *subject* and some appropriate *information* sources.
- But underlining its keywords won't deliver any of them.
- If all of the questions that you were likely to meet could be categorised according to their task, and if an explanation was offered on how to respond to the questions in each category, then you could ascertain how to handle a particular question by simply identifying the group to which it belonged and following the accompanying guidance. That guidance could also include suggestions on how best to structure the essay.
- If you were also given advice on how to treat the title's subject and where to find information relevant to your work, you would then have all four of the things you needed to know: task, outline, subject and information sources.

- This book shows you how to uncover all four things on the TOSI list using a three-stage process.

Mini-outline: An essay plan that's summarised in five or six bulleted sentences.

CHAPTER 3
TASKS THAT LEAD TO AN OUTLINE

Introduction to tasks

When I talk about an essay question's 'task', I'm referring to the job that it asks a student to do. In theory, lecturers could set dozens of different kinds of tasks. But in practice, they tend to stick to some old favourites which fall into seven categories:

- Comparison
- Evaluation
- Explanation
- Definition
- Description
- Interpretation
- Discussion

You'll be able to identify which of these categories a specific question belongs to by comparing it with the example questions given in this book. And once you have found a match and identified your question's task type, you'll be given further information which explains what that task expects you to do; for example, "determine the causes or reasons for a particular outcome."

But establishing the task tells you more than what you're supposed to do; it can also give you a strong indication of how the essay might be laid out. After all, you'll want your work to be organised into a structure which leads the reader *logically* through the steps of your thought process.

Tasks that lead to an outline

The guidance given for the first four task types will help you to construct a suitable arrangement for your assignment, as it will include suggested outlines for those tasks. However, the last three task types are what I call *unpredictable*; their freeform, open-ended nature means that it's just not possible to define a 'correct' outline for them. For those tasks, it will be up to you to formulate your own essay structure, although you'll be given some strategies for doing this. The unpredictable tasks will be covered in the next chapter, "Tasks that don't lead to an outline".

Course affects task

Before I introduce each of the task types, it's worth noting that your approach to a question will be different depending upon whether you are studying a science subject or an arts and humanities subject. Your course will decide whether or not you'll get the opportunity to derive your own conclusions from evidence. In other words, building a case.

Generally speaking, science titles will not be asking for *your* opinion on an issue, but will expect you to relay your knowledge of *your discipline's* current understanding of the subject. This is why undergraduate science assignments rarely ask for an evaluation, a subjective definition, an interpretation or a discussion. Descriptions, explanations and comparisons are much more common and will inevitably expect essays which reflect the established way of thinking.

However, some engineering or technology lecturers may occasionally ask students to present an argument if their classes are concerned with the social effects of the course. For example: "Discuss the tenet that in the future, computer crime will have a major effect on society." (Information Systems)

By contrast, arts and humanities courses give students a much greater opportunity to put forward their own ideas about a subject, and this opens up the entire range of possible task types.

So without any further delay, let's meet the first category.

Task 1: Comparison

What are you being asked to do?

Comparison questions ask you to identify the characteristics that are either shared or not shared by two or more things and assess their significance. In a nutshell, "What are the interesting areas of similarity and/or difference?"

How do you identify these questions?

The most obvious identification marks for such titles are the words 'compare' and 'contrast' and you can see these in the following questions:

> "Compare and contrast the Late Neolithic activity in the Avebury region in Wiltshire and the islands of Orkney." (History and Archaeology)
>
> "Compare and contrast computational and ecological approaches to perception." (Cognitive Science)
>
> "Compare and contrast astronomy and astrology." (Astronomical Science)

If these words don't appear, then an emphasis on multiple viewpoints can give away a comparison title. The next two questions show how plurals like 'accounts', 'theories' and 'views' encourage students to relate different perspectives to each other:

> "Which accounts and lay theories unite, and which divide contemporary 'feminisms'?" (Psychology)
>
> "Assess some different views of how the Mahayana arose from among tendencies and ideas found in the schools and practices of earlier forms of Buddhism." (Comparative Religion)

While an absence of command words will demand a closer look, there are times when misleading commands must be disregarded altogether to recognise the title beneath. The next three questions require you to see through the initial command words to the underlying task, which is given away by terms like 'similarities', 'differences' and references to *two* plays or *two* writers:

19

Tasks that lead to an outline

> "Discuss the similarities and differences in human and machine abilities to recognise and learn patterns." (Cognitive Science)
>
> "Explore the balance between external and internal factors affecting the central figures in two plays." (English)
>
> "In a consideration of two or three writers, assess the politics of poetry during the age of the democratic revolution." (English)

How do you respond?

In what way should you address these titles? A comparison essay will put two or more situations side by side, identify interesting differences or similarities and comment upon their significance. So a possible structure for your response could look like this:

- Introduction
- Outline subject 1
- Outline subject 2
- Discern the areas of common ground between these subjects
- Discern the areas of contrast between them
- Analyse these areas and assess their significance
- Conclusion, with your own judgement

Here's an alternative structure:

- Introduction
- Outline subject 1
- Outline subject 2
- Discern one particular area of commonality/contrast between subjects 1 and 2
- Discern a second area of commonality/contrast between subjects 1 and 2
- Discern a third area of commonality/contrast between subjects 1 and 2
- Analyse the similarities/differences with some assessment of their significance
- Conclusion, with an expression of your own position on the matter

Note: These structures are only suggested starting points for your work. Please don't assume that these basic outlines represent the only way of doing things.

Task 2: Evaluation

What are you being asked to do?

Evaluation questions ask you to evaluate the accuracy of a statement by judging how well it is supported by evidence. After examining the proposition, you may fully agree, fully disagree, or more usually, hold a view somewhere in between.

How do you identify these questions?

Because they often contain a quote or a viewpoint, these questions can be quickly identified. The most recognised form that this type of question takes is, "Here is a statement. Discuss." Here are some examples:

> "Neural networks are merely statistical pattern recognisers. Discuss." (Computer Science)
>
> "The typography used on packaging is as important as the visual elements. Discuss." (Design)
>
> "School plays a vital role in children's cognitive development. Discuss." (Psychology)

And there are variations on this theme:

> "'In object-orientated terminology, workflow is an instance of the general class of groupware systems'. Argue this." (Computer Science)
>
> "'Computer graphics are just an expensive alternative to pens and paper.' Aren't they?" (Graphic Design)

A rearranged and less stark format begins with a phrase like "Examine the view..." or "Assess the claim..." shown in these questions:

> "Discuss the tenet that in the future, computer crime will have a major effect on society." (Information Systems)
>
> "Assess the proposition that American Dramatists were more radical than their audiences and had to disguise their true messages." (English & American Studies)
>
> "Examine the view that religious ideas and institutions are necessarily conservative forces." (Comparative Religion)

Tasks that lead to an outline

Questions that ask for a quantity on a sliding scale are also part of this group. They might start with "To what extent", "To what degree" or "How far can it be said":

> "To what extent did Americans look to the past rather than the future for answers to current problems? How far were figures such as Thoreau or Emerson, Whitman or other radical writers the precursors of '60s culture?" (English & American Studies)
>
> "How revolutionary was the American Revolution?" (History)
>
> "How reliable is Herodotus as a source for early Greek history?" (Classics & Ancient History)

A question that can be answered with a 'yes' or a 'no' or that gives another two alternatives falls into this group. Again, it is unlikely you'll be in complete agreement with either extreme:

> "Must scientific explanations always give causal information?" (Philosophy)
>
> "Does the beginning of the Neolithic mark an abrupt change in subsistence and society or was it a more gradual process?" (History and Archaeology)
>
> "Is language learned or is it innate? Use recent evidence to support your answer." (Psychology)

Exceptions

You must beware of questions that contain quotes but which *don't* belong in this category. The following questions use quotes just to "set the scene", *without* asking your opinion of those quotes:

> "'The future of computing will be wearable computers, integrating sensor information from a technologically-enhanced environment.' 'The future of computing is the network.' What is your view of the future of computing?" (Computer Science)
>
> "'The Text is plural' (Barthes). In what ways can literary texts be understood to have multiple meanings?" (English Literature)

How do you respond?

However the title is put, your task is to examine the statement's consistency with the available evidence and present your own assessment of its credibility. So one suggestion for the structure of your response is this:

- Introduction
- Expand upon the statement given or the question asked in the title
- Provide the arguments and evidence that agree with the statement given or that adopt a particular position when answering the question
- Provide the arguments and evidence that disagree with the statement given or that adopt an alternative position in answer to the question
- Compare and evaluate the arguments that agree and disagree
- Conclusion (with your own judgement)

Here's an alternative structure:

- Introduction
- Expand upon the statement given or the question asked in the title
- Discern one particular area relevant to the statement given or question asked and assess it from alternate perspectives. (What do different viewpoints say about this single aspect of the statement/question?)
- Discern a second area relevant to the statement given or question asked and assess it from alternate perspectives
- Discern a third area relevant to the statement given or question asked and assess it from alternate perspectives
- Compare and evaluate all perspectives that agree and disagree
- Conclusion (with your own judgement on the matter)

Note: These structures are only suggestions for how you might organise your work and don't represent the *only* way of laying out your ideas!

Tasks that lead to an outline

Task 3: Explanation

What are you being asked to do?

Explanation questions take a fact or an event and ask you to give the reasons for that particular outcome. This is a task where you are given an effect and are asked to supply the cause(s).

How do you identify these questions?

Phrases which characterise explanation questions are 'explain', 'account for' and 'give reasons':

> "Explain the success of the Norman invasion of England in 1066." (English History)
>
> "Account for the breakdown in relations between Sparta and Athens. Consider both the sixth- and fifth-century evidence." (Classics & Ancient History)
>
> "Give reasons for the success of the Bolsheviks in October 1917." (Slavonic Studies)

But a good test for detecting explanation questions is if they can be reworded in the form "Something happened here. Why?" And this is precisely how the following questions are put:

> "Why did so many people in the 1960's think that radical change was necessary?" (Modern History)
>
> "Why did Britain colonise North America and why did she succeed?" (History)
>
> "Why has the organisation structure changed from its traditional hierarchical structure in the 1970s?" (Computing Science)

How do you respond?

What does an explanation essay look like? As with the description task type that I discuss later, questions from applied courses ask students to show their knowledge of the generally accepted explanation, rather than putting forth their own opinion.

In science and other applied subjects, the structure of an explanation assignment may only be a simple one-two-three list of steps for how a particular outcome is reached. But even so, students can still demonstrate to lecturers that they know what they're talking about, that they can write something that flows smoothly and that they can mention the small details which indicate to lecturers that they've done their research thoroughly.

However, arts and humanities questions require the student to piece together evidence, rationalising their *own* explanation for the outcome. The structure of such an essay must reach back to the events identified by the student as root causes to arrive at the outcome given in the title.

Explanation assignments have a predictable structure because they supply an effect that the causes can build toward. There is also ample opportunity to analyse each possible cause, weigh them up against each other and then give your own view on the most likely cause or combination of causes, together with counter-arguments.

Fundamentally, an explanation essay will corral an assortment of possible causes or reasons together in one assignment and logically test them to see just how influential each was on the outcome given in the question. For example:

- Introduction
- Outline possible cause 1
- Outline possible cause 2
- Outline possible cause 3
- Logically explore how much influence each of the possible causes could have had on the outcome
- Conclusion (with your own view on the matter)

Or for an alternative structure:

- Introduction
- Briefly outline possible causes 1, 2 and 3
- Discern one particular area of the outcome and assess how much influence was exerted by each of the possible causes
- Discern a second area of the outcome and assess how much influence was exerted by each of the possible causes

- Discern a third area of the outcome and assess how much influence was exerted by each of the possible causes
- Encapsulate which areas of the outcome were influenced by which causes
- Conclusion (with your own judgement of the most accurate explanation)

Note: These basic templates show the fundamental internal workings of the assignment, but you should modify them to suit the needs of your own work.

Task 4: Definition

What are you being asked to do?

The meaning of words or phrases is open to interpretation if it depends upon the context in which they are used and what they are applied to. A definition question will test your ability to explore all the aspects of such words or phrases.

How do you identify these questions?

Definition questions hinge on the meaning of words, and so they'll sometimes begin with "What do you understand by...?" or "What does somebody mean by...?" For example:

> "What does Marx mean by 'alienation'?" (Social Studies)

The following philosophy questions can be answered with a 'yes' or a 'no' but are only partly evaluation questions. Students must explore the meaning of the central terms before they can be satisfactorily answered:

> "Can we experience necessity?" (Epistemology)
> "Can a virtuous person fail to achieve happiness?" (Ethics)

How do you respond?

The meaning of the words at the heart of the title must be explored. However, at undergraduate level, you will not be expected to derive your own definition of a word from fundamental principles; instead, you'll do lots of research and cite references to other writers' interpretations. So rather than writing an essay that directly dissects the meaning of a word or phrase, it might be better to introduce a few existing interpretations of the word or phrase and test them against each other, where you can ask questions like "Which definitions are the most apt and why?" or "Does this definition apply to all instances of the word/phrase?"

Perhaps your essay might look like this...

- Introduction
- An overview of the various aspects of the word or phrase that is in the title
- Potential definition 'a' with an exploration of how well it interprets the word/phrase
- Potential definition 'b' with an exploration of how well it interprets the word/phrase
- Potential definition 'c' with an exploration of how well it interprets the word/phrase
- Comparative analysis of all definitions
- Conclusion, giving your preferred definition(s) with reasons for that choice

Or alternatively,

- Introduction
- An overview of existing definitions 'a', 'b' and 'c'
- First aspect of the word/phrase and some analysis of whether the existing definitions pertain to it
- Second aspect of the word/phrase and some analysis of whether the existing definitions apply to it
- Third aspect of the word/phrase and some analysis of whether the existing definitions are relevant to it
- Discussion of how well the available definitions apply to every aspect of the word/phrase in question
- Conclusion, giving your own view of the most accurate definition of the word/phrase in the title

Note: Again, these brief outlines are only suggestions for how to structure your essay. You're free to use these as a starting point and modify them to suit your own needs, but they aren't the only way to lay out your ideas!

Chapter summary

- The job that an essay title asks you to do usually falls into one of seven categories.
- A suitable essay structure can be predicted for four of the categories, but not for the remaining three.
- In the arts and humanities, essay questions will often ask you to construct your own unique answer. But this is very rare in the sciences.
- Comparison questions place two (or more) things side by side and ask you to examine why they are similar or different.
- Evaluation questions ask you to assess the accuracy of a statement using evidence to support your reasoning.
- Explanation questions focus upon an outcome and ask you to establish the reasons for it.
- Definition questions refer to a word or phrase and then ask you to investigate all aspects of its meaning.

Case-building: Constructing your own carefully reasoned answer to an essay question, using logic and evidence.

CHAPTER 4
TASKS THAT DON'T LEAD TO AN OUTLINE

Two kinds of tasks

At the start of this book, I said that university lecturers are more interested in how students think than what students know. This is why they set essay questions which require more than the reciting of facts. More precisely, there are specific things that lecturers expect to see when they're marking student assignments for arts or humanities courses:

- Your own answer to the question rather than a 'correct' answer taught in class
- A supporting case or argument which leads to that answer
- A structure for the essay which allows your argument to progress in logical steps
- The investigation of evidence with some analytical thinking and some critical thinking
- The inclusion of alternative views that counter-balance your own viewpoint
- Confident use of your discipline's specialist terms and jargon
- A tone of voice which is measured and dispassionate
- A properly formatted list of academic references at the end of your essay

Your job is to work out how to deliver all of these elements with only the title as a starting point.

But that's not quite as scary as it sounds, because figuring out how to provide those things becomes much easier when you can roughly sketch a plan for your essay as a five- or six-point mini-outline. And for the four tasks that you've already met, this isn't too difficult.

Why is that? The preceding four tasks all have some fixed, dependable aspects that you can rely upon when formulating your answer. For example, comparison questions always offer two (or more) distinct things that need to be compared. Evaluation questions inevitably offer a premise with which you will agree, partially agree or completely disagree.

Because those task types have certain features that are always present, it's possible to foresee where you'll get the opportunity to do all of that case-building, analysis and criticism that your lecturer will be looking for. From there, you can plan how the basic structure of the essay might look. And you can confidently anticipate all of this without knowing anything else about the question—you just have to identify the task type. That's why I call this first group "the predictable tasks."

However, there are seven task types in total. So what about the others?

When assigning any of the three remaining tasks, lecturers *still* want to see how students think. But for this second group, it's much harder to envision the rough outline of a prospective essay because the tasks themselves are far less pre-determined and much more open to interpretation; the structure of an essay written in response to one of these "*un*predictable tasks" is entirely at the discretion of the writer.

Although this sounds wonderfully liberating, it actually means that an unpredictable task won't provide some of the helpful indicators that a predictable task would. For example...

- A point that clearly needs to be proved or disproved
- Where your opportunity is to build a case
- An indication of where you need to apply some analytical thinking (pulling things apart to examine why they are significant or how they are connected to other things)
- An indication of where you need to apply some critical thinking (assessing the merits and faults of evidence, examples or arguments)

- Any other clues to building a suitable essay structure

In other words, your lecturer wants to see you analysing, criticising, case-building and point-proving—but when the task is unpredictable, it shows no obvious way to deliver these things.

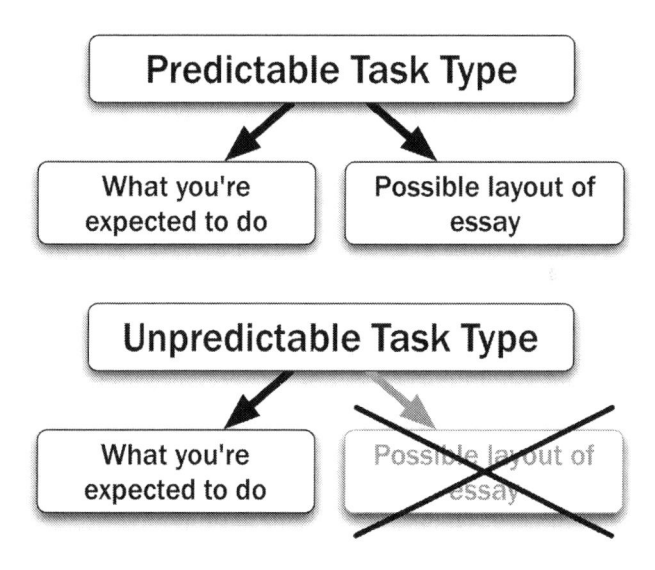

Predictable Task Type
- What you're expected to do
- Possible layout of essay

Unpredictable Task Type
- What you're expected to do
- ~~Possible layout of essay~~

If the task doesn't tell you how the finished essay might look, an exploration of the subject is your only hope. This means that it's the *next* two stages which must deliver something that you expected to learn from this stage. So while you're thinking about your question's subject and gathering information in the library, you'll also need to look for clues that suggest ways to structure your work in a coherent and logical way.

For this reason, the "How do you respond?" sections of the three remaining tasks will refer to the subject stage and the information stage of the decoding process before you've actually reached those parts of the book. While this is a little bit inconvenient, the strategies for tackling the remaining task types should still make sense.

Tasks that don't lead to an outline

Task 5: Description

What are you being asked to do?

On a science, technology, economics or similarly applied course, description questions are the simplest type of task. Such titles merely ask for an essay which presents evidence or conveys somebody else's findings. They make a straight request for existing information, and your response should demonstrate that you're familiar with that information and that you can create a well-written piece about it.

But if you're on an arts or humanities course, then matters aren't so straightforward; giving a description may not *seem* like a point-proving or argument-building exercise, but at university level, you would be asking for a low grade if you only handed in a scrapbook of facts to your lecturer. Description assignments will still need to display some analytical and critical thinking.

How do you identify these questions?

How do you spot a description question? Typical command words used are 'describe' or 'outline':

> "Describe the important techniques that are used in the construction of speech recognition systems." (Computer Science)
>
> "Outline the key features of the life of Siddhartha Gautama, setting him in his religious and social context." (Comparative Religion)
>
> "Describe how the expression of genes may be regulated in either bacterial or mammalian cells." (Pathology)

Description questions that don't use 'describe' or 'outline' are given away by sounding as though their answer might be in the form of a list:

> "What were the main ideas involved in 1960s Radicalism?" (Modern History)
>
> "What duties did citizenship entail in Athens and in Sparta?" (Classics & Ancient History)
>
> "What influences from psychoanalytical theory do you discover in American drama?" (English & American Studies)

Tasks that don't lead to an outline

Occasionally, some science titles use command words which can lead the reader into a case of mistaken identity. They are not asking for your own personal explanation of something; they are asking you to convey the scientifically accepted explanation or procedure. Because of this, it's possible to replace the first word in each of them with 'Describe' and find that they still have virtually the same meaning:

> "Explain how phonological segments are organised into syllables, giving examples from two different languages." (Linguistics)
>
> "Discuss as specifically as possible how you would measure the efficiency of the heart in the body." (Biology)
>
> "Explain how top-down design is used to solve a problem." (Computer Science)

Many pure and applied science questions are description questions irrespective of how they're worded. This is taken for granted to such a degree within science that some lecturers don't bother writing anything but a subject area. This is illustrated in the following questions:

> "Aluminium aerospace alloys." (Materials Science)
>
> "Impact craters within the solar system." (Astronomical Science)
>
> "Orbital angular momentum and spin in hydrogen and helium atoms." (Physics)

How do you respond?

How should someone respond to a description question? As with the other two unpredictable tasks, it's difficult to predict a single likely structure for every description assignment because the task itself is so open-ended.

Description questions often seem to be asking for a list of things, which suggests that the response should have a simple one-two-three structure—and if you're on an applied course, then that might be appropriate. But if you're on an arts or humanities course, then an essay which is nothing more than a laundry list padded out to fill a few thousand words is not going to get a very good grade. Your lecturers will want to see some

Tasks that don't lead to an outline

comprehension of the significance of the subject. Nonetheless, it can still be tough to deliver a complex response when the title you're facing has such simplistic demands.

So where can you look for assistance?

Strategy 1: Have you been given a combination question?

Description makes up only one part of an essay title when it's combined with another task such as explanation or evaluation. If that's the case, then you can look toward the *second* task to influence the structure of your assignment and to provide some opportunities for an argument, analysis and criticism. For example, the following question is a combination of a description task and an explanation task:

> "It is quite obvious that diplomacy failed to prevent World War II. Describe what diplomatic manoeuvres were made by the various powers which eventually went to war and explain why these diplomatic manoeuvres failed." (History of Western Civilisation)

There are other examples of combination questions later in this chapter, in the section called "Variations on the seven tasks". If there is no secondary task, it might be the title's *subject* that supplies the clues which help you to create a more substantial outline for your assignment.

Strategy 2: Have you been given unsubtle hints about your question's subject?

The following title resembles a combination title in that it asks more than one question:

> "Describe the history of the ancient Romans. Identify the major stages in ancient Roman history. What were the Romans' major accomplishments? What were their major shortcomings? What legacy did they leave for western civilisation?" (Ancient History)

But in this case, students are not being asked to do a number of *different* tasks; the extra questions are giving hints on how to answer that initial description task. For more information, refer to "Other things to spot" in the next chapter, "Developing the subject."

Strategy 3: See if the subject can be viewed from a second aspect.
Description assignments have titles that seem to ask for a list of things. You know that you'll have to discuss the events/characters/ideas that the title has specified, but if you can also describe the context/setting/background stuff going on at the same time, then you'll get a chance to assess the relationship/harmony/discord between the list of things and their context. See "A question's subject can have more than one aspect—and that's good news" in the next chapter.

Strategy 4: See what some preliminary research uncovers.
Life becomes easier when preliminary reading uncovers clues that offer ideas for structure and content. There's more about this in chapter six, "Finding sources of information."

Task 6: Interpretation

What are you being asked to do?
Interpretation questions ask you to explain the meaning of an author's work. One or more passages of text need to be deconstructed and expanded upon to spell out the message, significance and consequences of the work (or works) in your own words.

As you might imagine, answering an interpretation question relies heavily upon a skill that I've mentioned before: analytical thinking. You'll recall that analysis is all about pulling things apart to establish how they function, why they are significant or how they connect to other things. But you will also see the word 'critical' used in these questions, for example "Give a critical analysis..." Such questions are asking students to go further than mere examination to assess the merits, the faults, the effectiveness, the power or the prescience of the work. In other words, you'll have to create an argument to articulate your own viewpoint.

Tasks that don't lead to an outline

How do you identify these questions?

Interpretation questions are often found in literature courses and are marked out by phrases such as "Present a critical account" or "Write a critical analysis." Take a look at the following:

> "Write a critical analysis of one of the poems from *Lyrical Ballads*, taking into account Wordsworth's comments in *The Preface*."
> (English)
>
> "James Joyce's writing 'is not about something, it is that something itself', said Samuel Beckett. Explain what you think he meant, and to what extent this might equally be said of Beckett's own writing. Make detailed reference to *Dubliners* and *Waiting for Godot*."
> (English Literature)

How do you respond?

As with the description questions, it's hard to define a 'one-size-fits-all' response for a task as open-ended as interpretation.

Strategy 1: Can you find a context for this work?

Just as with description titles, it's possible that you could fall into the trap of creating a padded-out list when answering an interpretation question: "Line one of the poem means this... Line two of the poem means... Line three..." and so on. In the interests of producing a more mature and engaging thesis, you need to answer the question in a way that links its subject to a bigger picture. And this is where you might be able to talk not only about the author's work, but also about the *context* of the work as a second aspect of the subject: what motivated the work, what shaped the work and what gives the work its significance.

- *Were the events of the day the context of the work?* Is it important to frame the author's work within its historical period? Were there political struggles or social changes at the time that impacted the author's work?
- *Is the author's situation the context of the work?* Can you relate the author's work to his/her personal circumstances, the work of rival authors or the author's view of the world?

- *Is the audience the context of the work?* You might be able to reword "What is the meaning of...?" as "What is this author/philosopher trying to convey?" So is the author's relationship with his audience the second aspect of the subject? What assumptions has the author made about the audience? Is there something they don't know that his/her work tells them? Is there a prevalent way of thinking that the author is trying to challenge?

Strategy 2: Can you find an existing debate to engage with?

Another danger when answering an interpretation question is that you deliver a pompous lecture containing nothing but your own isolated opinion. This would be considered poor academic practice, since it fails to acknowledge the work of other critics or connect with their viewpoints. However, once you undertake some preliminary reading, you will encounter writers and views that your work can engage with and you will spot opportunities to analyse and weigh up their arguments. This gives you the chance to compose an essay that is connected rather than isolated.

Task 7: Discussion

What are you being asked to do?

Discussion questions can be the hardest to identify and answer, which is odd because the word 'discussion' is quite disarming. It evokes an image of friends with cups of coffee sitting around a table and chatting aimlessly. But this is part of the problem. When inspecting an essay title, you're looking for strong, decisive words that give you a clear indication of what is being asked for and 'discussion' is a vague, hazy kind of activity. The other unpredictable tasks might not provide you with a structure for the final essay, but at least 'describe' or 'interpret' gives you an indication of the job that you're supposed to do; discussion titles don't even give you that.

Tasks that don't lead to an outline

How do you identify these questions?

Command words which identify discussion titles are 'discuss', 'explore', 'examine' and 'assess'. Examples of these are shown here:

> "Discuss the methodological problems that the historian faces when working on Aksumite history." (African Studies)
>
> "Examine the relationship between ownership of the mass media and control over the media's output." (Sociology)
>
> "Explore the ways in which American dramatists both subverted and utilised the conventions of theatre before the end of WWII." (American Drama)
>
> "Assess the role of colour in packaging." (Design)

An absence of command words makes it difficult to identify a question's task. So the following are probably best classified as discussion titles after being eliminated from the other six types:

> "What did the experience of protest reveal about the nature of power and authority in the United States? Use events from campus life and from political protests such as the Chicago Democratic Convention." (American History)
>
> "What are the politics of place in *Mansfield Park?*" (English Literature)
>
> "How does *Lord of the Flies* symbolise the degradation of society?" (Modern Literature)

How do you respond?

How should you reply to a discussion title? This is the most open-ended task of all, since discussion titles do not ask for a single, clear objective as the previous six tasks do. Furthermore, such questions give little or no guidance on structuring an answer. This very relaxed form frees the student to not only set the essay's format, but also its objective (e.g. to compare two policies, to evaluate a policy's success, to explain a policy's outcome, etc.). So when responding to a discussion title, there are a lot of choices to make.

The range of strategies is very similar to those for a description task:

Strategy 1: Have you been given a combination question?

If so, the additional task will influence the shape of the discussion. See the next section, "Variations on the seven tasks."

Strategy 2: Have you been given unsubtle hints about your question's subject?

You should pay extra attention to any hints that nod towards a particular approach when shaping the essay. See "Other things to spot" in the next chapter.

Strategy 3: Try to see if the subject can be viewed from a second aspect

Can the subject of the question be split into more than one aspect? If so, you have much more to talk about and the prospect of some interaction between the two aspects becomes a possibility. See "A question's subject can have more than one aspect—and that's good news" in the next chapter.

Strategy 4: See what some preliminary research uncovers

Useful pointers to help you plan a structure for your assignment will come from preliminary reading, which I discuss in chapter six, "Finding sources of information."

———

And that completes the seven types of task.

If you'd like a method to help you to remember them all, they can be rearranged so that the first letter of each of the seven categories spells the word DECIDED.

Tasks that don't lead to an outline

Variations on the seven tasks

The "seven task" model applies to the vast majority of essay titles, but it isn't infallible. There are some variations that need extra work: combination questions and muddled task questions.

Combination questions

Combination questions ask students to undertake more than one task. These aren't unusual thanks to some common combinations like "describe and explain" or "describe and discuss." Here are some examples:

> "What is 'social responsibility in design'? Give some examples of socially responsible design which show different approaches to social responsibility. To what extent are designers able to operate in socially responsible ways?" (Communication Studies)
>
> "Describe the religious disputes of the fifteenth century and discuss how Zara Yaqob tried to resolve them and to what extent he was successful or not." (African History)
>
> "Explain the karma-rebirth perspective of Buddhism, clarify how this relates to Nibbana, and assess the role of ghosts and gods in the beliefs and practices of Theravada Buddhists." (Eastern Religions)
>
> "Both diplomacy and war were the tools which forged modern Italy. Describe the course of events of diplomacy and war which led to the formation of Italy. Also make some overall judgement about the effect that the way in which Italy was formed had on its subsequent history." (History of Western Civilisation)

These combination questions are good news when you're trying to plan your response, since they provide a clear picture of what your lecturer expects the assignment to deliver.

Muddled task questions

The overwhelming majority of essay questions can be categorised as asking you to complete one kind of task or another. But very rarely, you'll come across strange hybrid titles which are difficult to assign to a single category because they are open to a number of possible interpretations. Let's have an example:

> "In what ways, if at all, have the arrival of the 'information age' and the collapse of the state-socialist economies affected the nature of global politics?" (Political Science)

Without the words "if at all", this question would be asking for a list, and so you could categorise it as a description question. But *with* those words, there's the kind of yes/no decision that you might find in an evaluation question. So which one is it, and how do you respond? Your best course of action might be to note down all possible interpretations and reserve a final judgement until you've conducted some preliminary research. You can then choose the task that seems to represent the most appropriate approach and sketch out a rough structure accordingly. It might be that a hybrid structure is best suited to this hybrid task.

Let's have another example:

> "'Some felt the Victorian Age to be one of dynamic progress: others a world hastening to twilight and decay.' Consider the contrast referred to, as exemplified in the literature of the period. Include reference to at least three poets." (English)

This question doesn't quite fit into an existing mould, as it contains two opposite viewpoints within its quote, making it impossible to agree or disagree. The term 'contrast' might encourage you to answer it as a comparison question or the command word 'consider' may steer you toward treating it as a discussion. Again, preliminary research would help you to decide which approach is best.

Chapter summary:

- There are seven types of task that you might be asked to complete. Alas, for three of them, you won't be able to predict how the responding essay will be structured.

- But even without a structure to guide you, you'll still be expected to build a case or prove a point. You can never hand in a few pages of waffle.
- So for these remaining three tasks, you'll have to design your own essay structure based upon your analysis of the question's subject and the information you'll uncover later.
- Description questions ask you to present evidence or convey someone else's findings. But on an arts or humanities course, you'll still need to demonstrate analytical and critical thinking.
- Interpretation questions ask you to explain the meaning of an author's work in your own words.
- Discussion tasks are the hardest to respond to because they don't even offer a clearly defined task, let alone a suggested outline. They are the most open-ended of the seven types.
- Rarely, you'll find essay questions which can't be pinned down to a particular task type. Combination questions ask you to complete more than one kind of task. Muddled task questions straddle the boundary between individual task types.

CHAPTER 5
DEVELOPING THE SUBJECT

Introduction to subjects

The previous stage of the process was quite involved, so let's just have a quick recap to see where we are. There are four things that you need to know from an essay title: the **task** to perform, a rough **outline** for your essay, the **subject** to focus upon and an idea of the **information** sources that you'll need. Now that you've established the question's task, you should at least know what you're being asked to do and perhaps have an idea of how your assignment could be structured. And this brings us to the stage where you'll identify and develop the question's subject.

What is there to say about a title's subject? After all, it's easy to identify the subject of most assignment questions: Maslow's Theory of Needs, the causes of the Spanish civil war, the legacy of Modernist art and so on. There doesn't seem to be much more to know, and there probably isn't if you're on a hard science course, a technology course or some economics or business courses. You can take the subject at face value without the need to dig any deeper.

Likewise, if you're on an arts, humanities or soft science course, an essay question's subject should be just as easy to discern. However, there will be times when you can—and should—read more into it.

And so this stage contains a few ideas for extracting as much information as possible from a title's subject. Not all of the ideas will apply to every question, but this should still serve as a useful bag of tools to squeeze out every possible ounce of help.

A question's subject can have more than one aspect—and that's good news

If you're on an applied course learning a science, technology or business subject, then your essays are very likely to:

- Be based upon one of a limited set of tasks (primarily description and explanation)
- Have a fairly straightforward structure
- Demonstrate your understanding of an already established doctrine, rather than conveying your own original thoughts on a subject
- Have a word limit that gives just enough space to relay your knowledge

So that's quite straightforward. However, there is a different set of characteristics for assignments that are given to students on arts or humanities courses...

- The essay could be based upon any one of seven tasks
- It may or may not have a clearly predictable outline
- It will need to demonstrate your analytical and critical abilities to a university standard and ultimately deliver your own conclusion
- It could have a word limit of as many as three thousand words or more

This second set of characteristics are less constrained, and so the kinds of assignments that you could be asked to write cover a much broader range of possibilities, from "clearly defined task, predictable structure and easily achieved" to "unsure of the task, unable to predict the best structure and a tough job to finish."

At the most forgiving end of this spectrum are comparison questions. Whenever you're presented with a comparison title, the question will clearly split the subject into *two aspects* to explore and compare. For example:

Developing the subject

> "Compare and contrast the Iron Age of East Yorkshire and Wessex." (Prehistory)
>
> "Compare and contrast computational and ecological approaches to perception." (Cognitive Psychology)
>
> "Compare and/or contrast Russian society in the 1920s and in the 1930s." (Slavonic Studies)
>
> "In a comparative discussion of Edmund Burke and Tom Paine, say who has the better of the argument about the French Revolution, and give your reasons." (English Literature)
>
> "Compare and/or contrast European imperialism in the nineteenth century with American imperialism in the twentieth century." (Modern History)

Having a task that's clearly defined and a subject that can be viewed from two angles is enormously helpful when outlining the structure of your assignment, because it means that you can take a reasonable first guess at how you're going to respond:

1. Talk about the subject from the first aspect
2. Talk about the subject from the second aspect
3. Analytically discuss what they have in common and what sets them apart
4. Critically assess these similarities and differences
5. Draw to a close with your own personal conclusion

The fact that you even *have* this basic five-point outline is great news in itself, since it provides you with some kind of embryonic framework upon which to build your full-blown essay. But it's especially reassuring when you realise that the chance to discuss the subject from *two* aspects makes it easier to deliver those 'arts & humanities' characteristics mentioned above: a demonstration of analytical and critical thinking and a length that might stretch to three-thousand words.

So, comparison titles are a welcome sight because they always give you two aspects of a subject, and this makes life easier when answering a question. But is it only comparison titles that can help in this way? Or are there other occasions when you can find two aspects to a question's subject?

Developing the subject

Broad and narrow aspects (e.g. general vs. particular, detail vs. overview, events vs. context)

Sometimes, a question will invite students to look for a link between the specific and the general, and you can treat those two as separate aspects of the title's subject. You must also note in which direction the link goes.

For example, the following questions are asking you to provide the specific instances that either support a general theory or exemplify a general set of circumstances supplied by the question:

> "What evidence do we have for the changing nature of contact between Britain and the continent in the first millennium BC?" (Prehistory)

If I rewrite that question to emphasise the general and particular aspects, then it becomes:

> "What *specific* evidence do we have for the *generally* changing nature of…"

Here's another example:

> "How might women's writing in the Romantic period be described as 'revolutionary'?" (English Literature)

And again, this assignment will need *specific* examples of women's writing that might uphold the *general* description of the genre as 'revolutionary'.

Here's one more where you're being given a *general* situation (industrial depression and slump) and are being asked to provide the *specific* effects of that:

> "What were the effects on society in South Wales mining communities of the industrial depression and slump of the 1920s and 1930s?" (Welsh History)

Now in the following questions, the link between general and particular goes the other way; you are being asked to provide a general theory or backdrop as a context for the specific events or examples supplied by the question:

> "What in your opinion is the significance of the Merthyr riots of 1831?" (Welsh History)
>
> "Place one poem from *Lyrical Ballads* in historical context." (English Literature)

Time-related aspects (e.g. then vs. now, early vs. late, actions vs. consequences, before vs. after)

You can encounter subjects whose two aspects are time-related. Within each of the following three titles, you should be able to see "cause and effect":

> "In what sense do the changes in settlement practice in the second millennium BC result in the appearance of a domestic landscape?" (Prehistory)
>
> "Explain the effect that the Scientific Revolution had on the Enlightenment." (History, Western Civilisation)
>
> "In what ways can the events of Tewodros II's reign be said to premise his subsequent image as the 'father' of the modern state of Ethiopia?" (African History)

And the next three titles also have subjects that are viewed from two separate viewpoints in time:

> Then and now: "Explore the changes in the urban environment in the 1960s and assess contemporary ideas about city life and urban change." (Social Studies)
>
> Cause and cure: "What caused the Great Depression? What ended the Depression? Consider the examples of the United States and Germany." (Modern History)
>
> Intended and actual outcome: "The course of World War I in its first three months did not go as the Germans had planned. Explain both the German war plans for victory and the reasons why such well-laid plans did not work." (Modern History)

Developing the subject

Geographical aspects

Rather than coming up with a single list of duties common to both Athens *and* Sparta, two aspects are created when a separate list is made for each city. It's then possible to make comparisons:

> "What duties did citizenship entail in Athens and in Sparta?" (Ancient History)

And again in the following question, it's possible to imagine the answer as a single list of Western-focused reasons, but students would have more to work with if they view the war from both sides of the Iron Curtain.

> "Examine the reasons for the West's 'victory' in the Cold War." (Modern History)

Miscellaneous examples of "A versus B"

You will also find non-comparison questions with aspects that don't fit into a pre-determined category:

> "'The typography used on packaging is as important as the visual elements.' Discuss." (Design)
>
> "Explain how on the one hand Napoleon brought to fruition and implementation many of the goals of the French revolution, but on the other hand frustrated and refused to implement many other goals of the original revolutionaries." (History, Western Civilisation)

More than two aspects

This section has referred to many questions with two aspects to their subject, but sometimes they contain more than two:

> "'Religion has an important sociological role within British society.' Discuss this statement with particular reference to the theories of Marx, Durkheim, Weber and Comte." (Sociology)
>
> "Explain the differences in thought on the role of government and the individual in divine absolutism, limited government and Rousseau's ideas about the social contract." (History, Western Civilisation)

What if you can't see more than one aspect or perspective?

In the previous section, I summarised the circumstances that apply when a student is planning to write an essay for an arts or humanities course:

- The assignment could be based upon any one of seven tasks
- It may or may not have a clearly predictable structure
- It will need to demonstrate your analytical and critical abilities to a university standard and deliver your own conclusion
- It will have a word limit of as many as two or three thousand words

And I observed that, of all the types of questions you could be asked on such a course, comparison questions make life easiest when trying to satisfy the last three constraints on that list.

But what's at the other end of the scale? What kind of questions might give the *most* difficulty as you try to work within those same constraints? Well, if comparison questions offer a clearly predictable outline and a subject with at least two aspects, then the very opposite must be a question *without* a clearly predictable outline and a subject with only *one* apparent aspect. The situation is best illustrated with an example:

"What were the main ideas involved in 1960s Radicalism?"

You can see that this title's answer might be in the form of a list, so it's probably best treated as a description question. But since that's an unpredictable task, it offers no suggestions for the kind of structure that someone might use when composing the reply. And although it does have an easily identifiable subject—the main ideas of 1960s Radicalism—there is apparently no choice of aspects from which to view it. Anyone who fails to find another aspect will only be able to discuss that subject from a single viewpoint.

Developing the subject

If that happens, let's see how much there is to talk about:

> **The dominant ideas of 1960s radicalism**
> - Anti-materialist ecology movement
> - Anti-war movement
> - Challenge to race discrimination
> - Challenge to gender discrimination
> - Challenge to homosexual discrimination
> - Support for revolutionary left-wing politics

Hmmm. This may be a list of six relevant themes, but it isn't enough to base an essay upon. Or at least, not one that you would dare to hand in:

1. Of course you could enlarge upon and explain each of the items in this list. But conjuring up a three-thousand-word assignment is going to be a struggle if the only strategy is to pad out six bullet points.
2. There's no opportunity to demonstrate your analytical and critical abilities, because there's nothing upon which to build any kind of discussion or debate. Nor do you get the chance to conclude the work by giving your own personal position on the subject, because you've only listed a bunch of facts. Your assignment would read like a laundry list, and then your lecturer would hand back your work with the words "So what?" scribbled at the end.
3. With so little material to work with and no opportunity for analysis, you cannot plan any kind of feasible structure for this essay—other than the aforementioned laundry list.

The problem can be neatly summed up: by discussing one list of items in isolation, you've no opportunity to examine, describe, explain or evaluate their characteristics in relation to any other reference points.

Developing the subject

So as a contrast, let's examine a title with an easy-to-spot subject and *two* readily identifiable aspects:

> "Discuss the similarities and differences in human and machine abilities to recognise and learn patterns."

Since the title asks students to focus on "similarities and differences", you can identify this as a comparison task. And the subject of the assignment is "the ability to recognise and learn patterns"—but the question asks students to see that subject from *two* aspects: the ability that humans have and the ability that machines have. From the essay writer's point of view, this is great news!

Now that you can discuss the subject from the human angle *and* the machine angle, the amount of material to contribute to the assignment seems to have doubled. But in fact, the news is even better. Because you've been asked to examine "similarities and differences" between those two aspects, you can create interaction between them as you talk about what they have in common and what sets them apart, so whole new avenues open up to enrich the discussion. The amount of material that you can generate has now more than doubled, *and* you get the opportunity to lay out your own analysis and express your own opinion.

Now, let's go back to the title with *apparently* only one aspect:

> "What were the main ideas involved in 1960s Radicalism?"

Instead of looking at the events of the 1960s from a single perspective, let's take a moment to think about the main ideas of 1960s Radicalism in some sort of context. Radicalism gained its name from the degree to which it opposed the norms and conventions of *mainstream* culture. So if you use mainstream culture as a second lens through which to view the title, you could write an assignment that describes not only the ideas of 1960s Radicalism, but also involves the ideas of 1960s mainstream culture (second column below). And then you could talk about how different they were and why they clashed (third column). Fantastic!

Developing the subject

The dominant ideas of 1960s radicalism	The dominant ideas of the 1960s mainstream	Possible questions on how the two interact
• Anti-materialist ecology movement • Anti-war movement • Challenge to race discrimination • Challenge to gender discrimination • Challenge to homosexual discrimination • Support for revolutionary left-wing politics	• A culture of materialist aspiration • Acceptance or support of foreign wars • Mistrust of racial integration • Traditional view of "a woman's role" • No/limited tolerance of homosexuality • Cold War hostility to left-wing politics	• Did mainstream culture give birth to radicalism? • Why did radicalism reject the mainstream? • Was this an intergenerational conflict? • Was this ultimately about conformity versus individuality? • Did radicalism affect the direction of mainstream culture?

If you don't want to think contextually, you could think in *chronological* terms when looking for two perspectives, and write a composition which compares the world *before* and *after* 1960s Radicalism, and perhaps asks whether its ideas achieved their goals.

Alternatively, you might think in *geographical* terms when looking for your second perspective, by remembering that Radicalism wasn't only restricted to the streets and college campuses of the United States. You could then write an essay which introduces the ideas of European 1960s Radicalism, and which highlights the similarities and differences between the Radicalism of San Francisco and Paris.

Any of these three choices will give you much more material to contribute to the assignment and many more opportunities to show your lecturer that you've really thought about the issues, rather than just handing in a regurgitated list of things that you've read.

Other things to spot

I've discussed the advantages of finding more than one aspect to a question's subject. But the subject can also possess other characteristics that influence the way you plan your essay.

Are there any unsubtle hints about a subject's direction?

Lecturers sometimes write questions which include very clear signals that indicate what ground they expect the essay to cover. When you're planning a response, it's wise to ensure that your work is influenced by those unsubtle hints. In the first example below, students are not being asked to conclude their assignment with some old blurb about the goals of the revolutionaries. Rather, the two questions at the end of the title are very direct hints as to what the main thrust of the essay should consider:

> "Compare and/or contrast the Russian and Chinese revolutions. What were the goals of the Communists in each country? Did either Communist Party achieve its goals?" (Modern History)
>
> "Discuss how the ancients treated women, slaves and the poor. Was the treatment of these groups the same throughout the ancient world, or were there differences? Which of the ancient civilisations appear to have been closest to the early twenty-first century with respect to the treatment of women and the less privileged?" (Ancient History)
>
> "How did the world's economic system change during the twentieth century? You may want to consider some of the following developments: the Great Depression, globalisation, the consumer economy and the Internet." (Modern History)

Developing the subject

Are there any unfamiliar words or concepts that you're supposed to trip over and pay special attention to?

The appearance of unfamiliar terms is no accident—just like those unsubtle hints. In an essay question, an unusual word acts like a conspicuous rock that students are expected to look under. You can investigate this as the start point of your research:

> "One traditional view of Ethiopian civilisation speaks of a 'Semitic inheritance' as being a 'leaven' imposed on African soil. Discuss." (African History)
>
> "In what ways is technology 'gendered'?" (Social Studies)
>
> "What are 'mental accounts'? Is money fungible?" (Political & Social Psychology)

Is there a hidden agenda waiting to be discovered?

Occasionally, a question has a point to it that is only uncovered after some preliminary research. Your mission is to discover the hidden agenda and plan an essay that responds to it. For example, let's look at this question:

> "Compare and contrast the functions of NATO during the Cold War with the post-Cold War period." (International Relations)

This is a comparison question which, at first glance, asks the reader to put NATO's Cold War activities next to its post-Cold War activities, and write about anything of interest. But even a quick scan of related literature would reveal that NATO was devised to counter an attack from the colossal military machine of the Soviet bloc. With the demise of Communism, the Warsaw Pact disappeared, and so you can now see that the question's hidden agenda is to investigate whether NATO even *has* a purpose in a world where superpower arms races have been replaced by global terrorist networks.

On other occasions the agenda may not be a minor discrepancy that can be quickly cleared up, but an ongoing debate that's been rumbling on within your academic field for years. Your lecturers want you to stumble upon it and they expect you to engage with it.

Chapter summary

- The subject of a question is easy to identify. But that's not the end of the matter because there are good reasons for examining it more thoroughly.
- An essay question's subject might have more than one aspect. If it does, then writing an essay which fulfils your lecturer's expectations becomes easier.
- Comparison questions always divide their subject into two (or more) aspects.
- But other task types can also ask you to see a subject from two perspectives: a broad and a narrow aspect, time-related aspects, geographical aspects, etc.
- Finding more than one aspect makes it much easier to plan an essay. So it's worth trying to establish a second aspect, even if the question doesn't offer one.
- Questions can also contain "unsubtle hints" about a subject's direction and "hidden agendas" that you must discover.

CHAPTER 6
FINDING SOURCES OF INFORMATION

Introduction to preliminary reading

Your question has now been decoded to some extent. You know its **task** and its **subject**, and if the task was predictable, you'll have a provisional **outline** which will give you a good initial idea of how you might structure your essay. If the task wasn't predictable, then you still have some planning to do.

But whatever the situation, the next job is to extend your knowledge of the title's subject by reading introductory **information** about it. This is "preliminary reading."

What is it?

Preliminary reading is the kind of research that gives a broad overview of many things, rather than a deep understanding of one thing.

Why do it?

When you're writing an essay, there are constraints which affect the process:

- A deadline restricts the available time you have to complete the work.
- The work must be substantial enough to reach the set word limit.
- You must display a knowledge of your subject.
- Lecturers expect to see some indication that you've thought about the issues.

- You must convey those thoughts as a logical and coherent composition.

...and so on.

In response, you might want to create some kind of checklist to ensure that your essay meets these constraints—what information you must find, which viewpoints your essay could advocate, how much material you can expect to write, et cetera. And that's a great idea. But to do it, you'll need to have a good general overview of your area of study.

Preliminary reading is a time-efficient way of gaining that overview. You have to start your research somewhere, so you might as well begin in a place that's user-friendly, that builds your confidence and that gives you further information to guide your subsequent searches and reading efforts.

What do you need preliminary reading sources to provide?

Throughout the course of this book, there have been several occasions when I have said something like "Preliminary reading will improve your understanding of this" or "Preliminary research might uncover some helpful information here." It will be useful to bring all of those together in one place, as a reminder of all of the things that preliminary reading is expected to deliver.

Looking back over the process so far, you've already encountered the obvious situation where you can expect preliminary reading to help:

Preliminary reading's first chance to help: When completing the decoding of the title

- If the title's subject seems too limited in scope and one-dimensional, some cursory reading can uncover a second aspect to it, such as a context.

- On occasion, a question contains unfamiliar words or concepts that students are supposed to stumble upon and about which they must learn more.
- Sometimes, there is a point to a question that is only uncovered after some exploratory research.
- At other times, the question's subject can be part of an ongoing debate that you are supposed to discover and engage with.

But if we look forward to the next stages of the process, it's possible to foresee two more situations where preliminary reading will assist you...

Preliminary reading's second chance to help: When preparing for further research

- Preliminary reading gives you a broad overview of your academic discipline. This reveals its extents and all of the major features within, such as the key people, events, facts, theories, viewpoints and experiments—and their connections to each other. This is like having a map of the terrain that you are about to explore. You don't want your lecturer to return your essay and point out that you have completely ignored some important theory, prominent figure or influential event.
- But preliminary reading can also give you a broad overview of the *literature* of your discipline, introducing you to the most significant sources, whether they're likely to be helpful to you and in what way you can make use of them. This will save time from being wasted on inappropriate books, which is important when you're working to a deadline.
- During the course of preliminary reading, you'll be introduced to any specialist vocabulary that's peculiar to your discipline. This provides the opportunity to learn and understand these terms before you encounter them during your in-depth research.

Preliminary reading's third chance to help: When planning the essay structure

You've seen that there is a difference between predictable and unpredictable tasks.

Comparison, evaluation, explanation and definition tasks always set up the same kind of contentious situation that you must resolve or problem that you must figure out. This makes it possible to broadly predict your prospective essay's structure—which is a great help when you're brainstorming the kind of viewpoints that your argument could adopt.

However, if you're working with an unpredictable task, then you are given none of this: without having a clear point to prove or disprove, there's no need to build a case, analyse evidence or reach a judgement. It's impossible to predict such an essay's structure, because there's nothing to organise into a structure.

So how do you deal with this? How can you plan any kind of essay outline for an unpredictable task? The answer is to use preliminary research to *uncover* some area of debate in which your work can participate.

If you can just find something substantial with which your assignment can engage, then rather than writing an aimless, padded-out description or a woolly and meandering discussion, you can compose a piece with a *point* to it. Suddenly your work gains some direction, because if you can just establish a purpose for your essay, then it follows that you will have to build some kind of coherent, step-by-step train of thought to serve that purpose. And possible structures will emerge as you start to discover the various viewpoints that you could adopt and envision the kind of case that you can make. This is where preliminary reading is vital.

Where to go, what to do

Writing a "shopping list" of what to look for

So that's a general overview of what preliminary reading can deliver. But to pin down specifically what *your* essay needs, it might be an idea to make a shopping list of the exact questions you'd like your research sources to answer.

In the next chapter, the section entitled "What you finish with" will bring all of the information that can be gleaned from an essay title together into a single document. One of its headings will be called "What information am I hoping that preliminary reading will reveal?" and this is where you can note down that shopping list.

The range of information sources available for preliminary reading

With that shopping list close at hand, you can now start your research with some sense of purpose. You'll be looking for very general, introductory sources of information on your subject which give a broad overview of its major landmarks: background setting, main events, important theories, notable characters, prominent schools of thought, significant developments, and so on. And while reading these sources, you'll want to keep in mind the three objectives laid out above: decoding the title, preparing for further research and planning the essay structure.

So now the big questions are: What do you read? Where do you get all of this information?

Lecture Notes

This is a good place to start, since they're readily available to you and are likely to have some connection with the essay titles set by your lecturer. But remember, lectures don't supply all of the information that you need to know.

The Web

The Internet is great for giving a broad but shallow view of any subject, since it's widely available and searching for particular information is easy and very quick. But you'll need to remember that much of the information on the Web is not subject to academic peer review and you'll have to be careful how much weight you ascribe to Web articles. It will, however, provide some good leads to find more reliable sources.

Introductory Texts

The introductory textbook combines the accessible, informal nature of a Web article and the academic rigour of a substantial, traditionally published volume. These might be titled something like "An Introduction To..." and are designed to quickly and painlessly bring you up to speed on your chosen subject. To get suggestions for the best introductory texts available for your area of study, you will need to survey information sources such as the reading list supplied by your lecturer, your university library's catalogue, textbook bibliographies, lecturers' recommendations, fellow students' recommendations, your local bookstore, Internet bookstore listings (which sometimes include reviews and sample chapters), Web sites devoted to your subject and search engine results.

How do you know if you've found the right book? A good introductory book is one that gives you a broad, comprehensive overview of your course (including your question's subject area) in plain language, and is preferably recently published. Such books will be out there somewhere, and you need to find them!

Noting down your discoveries

Of course, when sources supply answers to the questions on your shopping list, you'll want to note them down. And once again, there's a space for this on the decoding sheet (also shown in "What you finish with"). Your notes don't have to be lines of text. It's perfectly okay to jot down diagrams, tables or bulleted lists to represent what you discover, if that gives a better understanding.

A deadline is looming and time is pressing on. So how do you know if you've done enough preliminary reading?

You'll know that you've done enough when your notes fulfil the three objectives in the "Why do we do it?" section above:

1. Do you now completely understand the title, what it wants you to do and any ulterior implications of what it's asking?

Have you been able to uncover all unknown terms, hidden agendas and ongoing debates alluded to by your question? Are you able to think about the essay question's subject from more than one aspect? And have all of these things been scribbled down?

2. Do you know enough about the main features of your subject to be able to pick out the sources most relevant to your assignment and understand them when you read them?

Before embarking upon targeted research of your title's subject, do you have a broad mental picture of the general area surrounding it? Does it contain all of the important events, ideas, people and achievements, their relationships and their significance? Equipped with this broad overview, can you now recognise and confidently read the in-depth texts that specifically relate to your question's subject?

3. Can you visualise at least one way (but preferably a few different ways) in which the course of your essay could be neatly summarised?

Preliminary reading might suddenly yield a credible structure for the essay. Have you noted this down as a provisional outline?

Okay, that's preliminary reading. How is in-depth research different?

So far, you've been trying to work out what an assignment question is asking you to do, before preliminary reading suggested a few possible ways in which you could do it. But at some point, you will have to commit to one of those ways.

Let's say that you've decoded a title's task, and that's great news because now you're able to positively identify what the question is asking—for example, it might want you to build an argument that compares two historical events or build a case which evaluates the accuracy of a statement. However, you still have to actually *build* that case, and this means deciding *which*

Finding sources of information

case you're going to build. Do you think that historical event 'A' was more influential than 'B'? Or was event 'B' the more significant influence? Do you think that the statement contained within the assignment question is accurate? Or is it hopelessly incorrect? Or somewhere in between?

As you can see, once you've established what you're supposed to do, you have to start thinking about how you'll actually *do* it. So with that in mind, in-depth research is the stage where you look out for the following:

- Vitally important to all assignments, you'll need to uncover evidence that has something to say about the title or makes a contribution to answering the question. Not only can you point to this evidence in your essay, but you can also provide your own critical analysis. For example, what does a particular piece of evidence tell you? How does it influence your view? How much significance does it carry in the overall picture? How far can it be trusted?
- If you've been given the kind of task that expects you to adopt a particular intellectual position and deliver your own judgement, it would be nice to be aware of the stances that other commentators have taken on the matter. Secondary sources can reveal the existing responses in academic literature to your question, which will show you a range of possible arguments and the options available for your own work.
- But in addition to merely reading other people's interpretation and analysis of the evidence, you can engage with those commentaries. Comparing your argument to that of others demonstrates that your work reaches out to existing literature, and quoting counter-arguments that disagree with your own planned argument will give academic balance to your essay.

Chapter summary

- You need the kind of information which will give you a good general overview of your subject. This is provided by preliminary reading.
- Preliminary reading can help you to finish the decoding of a title, prepare for further research and plan the outline of the essay.
- If you write a shopping list of the questions to which you need answers, you can pin down exactly what you want preliminary reading to deliver.
- Your lecture notes, the Internet and introductory texts are good places to start your research.
- When you find answers to your questions, you'll want to note them down.
- Preliminary research will reveal a few ways in which you could answer an essay title. Your in-depth research will influence which of those ways you commit to.

CHAPTER 7
CONCLUDING THE WHOLE PROCESS

What you finish with: The complete decoding sheet

Now that the parts of the TOSI process have been discussed individually, I'd like to put all of these pieces together and lay out everything that a student can expect to squeeze out of an essay title:

The original title:

Writing out the essay title to be decoded at the top of a blank page is an easy place to start.

(Stage 1: Task and Outline)

What's the task type?

Which characteristics of the title give clues about its task? And which of the seven tasks do they point towards?

Is there anything else to notice about the task?

Does the question comprise a combination of tasks? Is the question's task muddled?

Is the task predictable or unpredictable?

If the outline for this kind of task is predictable, then it can be written out here. But if it isn't, then you're going to have to look for clues to help you to create a suitable structure from scratch.

(Stage 2: Subject)

What's the question's subject?

What the essay is about should be easily identifiable and is usually defined by rewriting part of the title.

Is there more than one aspect to this subject?

Does the subject have another aspect (such as a context, a history, a counterpart or an opposite) that will help you to create an essay with a complex structure, rather than a one-dimensional laundry list?

Is there anything else to notice about the subject?

Can you spot any unsubtle hints which emphasise a certain area of the subject and push you to take the essay in that particular direction? Are there any unfamiliar words that you are supposed to pay attention to and follow up during your research? Can you detect any hidden agendas that you should stumble upon and engage with?

The same question rewritten in its decoded, expanded form:

Having looked up the title's task and dissected the title's subject, you should now be able to rewrite the demands of the title in a much fuller and more explanatory way.

Now that the task and the subject have been identified, is it possible to create a tentative outline that's tailored to this particular assignment question?

The rewrite of the original question will have spelled out exactly what it wants you to do. This means that the generic outline that was copy-and-pasted into 'Stage 1' above can now be modified so that it matches the demands of the question much more closely. This tailored outline will give you a firm idea of how many sections your essay will have and the job of each one.

(Stage 3: Information sources)

What information am I hoping that preliminary reading will reveal?

Before you conclude this decoding exercise, it would make sense to write down what you think you will need from your journey to the library. If you can decide what you need to know and which questions need answering at this stage, then you've got a starting place for your research. This is much better than staring uncomprehendingly at shelves of nondescript books. If there are specialist words to be looked up or agendas to be unearthed, then you can return to this sheet to fill in the blanks (see next question).

What did preliminary reading reveal?

This is the space left for the extra information or the better understanding you've gained from preliminary reading.

So what's the full story behind your assignment question? What are the main ideas, events and personalities of your question's subject area? Was there more to the title than you could have anticipated? Is there an unforeseen agenda hidden within it? If the question contained an unpredictable task, can you now envisage how you might structure your response so that you can build a case or work towards a definite conclusion?

So, what now?

This is the place to plan your next steps, based upon the answers to the preceding questions.

Is this decoding method infallible?

We've seen how this three-stage method can help to decode many, many essay questions. But is it infallible? Will it work with every question that you might meet? Alas, the answer is no. At the beginning of the Task-Outline stage, you saw that an assignment *usually* falls into one of seven groups. And the Subject stage contained a toolbox of ideas that would *generally* be helpful to make the most of a title's subject. This wording deliberately acknowledges those rare questions that won't neatly fit into a predetermined category.

So, suppose the worst case happens. What if you're given a question that doesn't seem to fit into any of the seven task groups or doesn't have a clearly recognisable subject? Let's confront such a nightmare:

> "In what does the distinction between 'left' and 'right' in politics consist?" (Political Science)

Okay, it might be better to start by identifying the subject. You might focus on the words "'left' and 'right' in politics" because they look like they sum up the subject of this question. And you can probably split that subject into two aspects, which means that you can talk about the 'left' and then you can talk about the 'right'. So that's promising.

But what isn't so encouraging is the unrecognisable nature of this question's *task*. How should someone categorise it? As it's not obvious, it's time to employ some reasoning by elimination...

- Is it an evaluation task? No, because you're not being asked to measure the accuracy of a statement against existing evidence.
- Interpretation? No again, because you're not required to express the meaning of someone else's work in your own words.
- Description? I don't think so; the question is asking you to do lots of digging around and weighing up and reasoning here—so it's much more involved than a simple description.

- Explanation? "Giving reasons for a particular outcome" feels promising, but this question has no sense of cause and effect.
- Definition? Yes, there's a little bit of that—but it's not so much asking you to define a single term as establish the *differences* in two definitions.
- So, "the distinction between 'left' and 'right'" means that it must be a comparison question, but with an emphasis on 'contrast'... right? Hmmm. That's getting close, but the words "In what does the distinction... consist?" mean that you're being asked to *define* what makes up the distinction—which brings you back to definition.

So by elimination, this task has been identified as being somewhere between definition and comparison. Perhaps you could rewrite the question as, "Define the core characteristics of the political 'left', do the same for the political 'right' and then compare the two to establish what fundamentally separates them." And that rewrite also serves quite well as a mini-outline for the course of the essay.

Let's imagine a second, uncomfortable situation. What if you're presented with a title which you simply can't understand because it contains unfamiliar terms or concepts? Here's a good example:

> "In what ways is the theatre re-theatricalised within Modernism?"
> (English Literature)

First, the good news: you can identify this question's task. "In what ways" asks for a list, so you can think of it as a description question—although that's still quite open-ended.

But what about the question's *subject*? What does it mean? Which theatre is the question talking about? What does 're-theatricalised' mean? How was it 'theatricalised' to begin with? What is the relationship to Modernism? And are there any other 'isms' that have re-theatricalised anything?

This short list has shown that although students can't always claim to know the answers, it is possible to pose some targeted questions. By asking them, you can use naiveté to your advantage to reveal the way forward: by bombarding the title with all of the questions that you have and recording them on paper as they come to you, you equip yourself with some great starting points for research. This approach keeps you working rather than sinking into despair. And from a confidence perspective, it also reminds you that while you may not know the answers, you *are* armed with the incisive questions.

Once you've created your list of questions, you can go to the library or search the Web and begin a little preliminary reading. This will probably unearth enough information to give you a toehold on the title.

If you still don't understand the essay question after employing this method, you can ask your lecturer for assistance. And rather than saying something vague like "I don't get it. What does this mean?", your previous work will allow you to pose more intelligent-sounding questions which show the lecturer that you've already made a serious effort to make sense of the title.

Chapter summary

- Everything you can elicit from an essay question can be placed together in a single document.
- A process of elimination can help when you're struggling to identify a title's task.
- A barrage of targeted questions can kick-start your research when you're struggling to understand a question's subject.

CHAPTER 8
WORKED EXAMPLES

Introduction to worked examples

I wrote this book in the hope that it would equip readers with a toolkit that could transform unfriendly, cryptic essay questions into a full understanding of what was being asked and a clear plan of action for achieving it. I also sprinkled as many example questions throughout the chapters as I could, to show how an otherwise dry and sterile theory can actually be used in real life.

With that in mind, I'd like to conclude with three fully worked examples that demonstrate how this three-stage technique decodes a title from start to finish. I've picked titles that include both predictable and unpredictable tasks and which reflect a range of course subjects. But I've also tried to ensure that these titles aren't too obscure and specialised, so that all readers can understand them.

I've written these examples in the first person to give the sense of looking over my shoulder while I show you how I would deal with them.

So now that that's cleared up, let's take a look at the example questions...

Worked examples

Example Question 1
Title:
"'The conditions that have created California's Silicon Valley are almost impossible to replicate anywhere else in the world.' Discuss." (Business Studies)

What's the task type?
The question consists of a provocative statement followed by a request for my response, so it's an evaluation question. This means that I'll be evaluating how well this statement is supported by evidence. It comes from a non-science subject, so I am expected to make and provide my own judgement on this subject, rather than recounting a widely accepted explanation.

Anything else to notice about the task?
It's not a combination of more than one task, nor is it muddled.

Is the task predictable or unpredictable?
As an evaluation question, the shape of the responding essay ought to be fairly predictable. I should be able to look up a suitable structure for this kind of task and use it as the starting point for creating my own outline for this particular question. One option looks like this:

- Introduction
- Expand upon the statement given (or the question asked) in the title
- Provide arguments with evidence that agree with the statement given or that adopt a position when answering the question
- Provide arguments with evidence that disagree with the statement given or that adopt an opposing position in answer to the question
- Compare and evaluate the arguments that agree and disagree
- Conclusion (with your own judgement)

Worked examples

What's the question's subject?
Whether it's possible or not to replicate the conditions that created Silicon Valley.

Is there more than one aspect to this subject?
I think that the most apparent way to see this question from more than one aspect is to divide the discussion between the conditions in Silicon Valley and the conditions in other parts of the world.

Is there anything else to notice about the subject?
I don't see any unsubtle hints on the direction of the assignment or any unfamiliar words that I'm supposed to trip over. And I'll only find out if there's a hidden agenda behind the question when I conduct some preliminary research.

The same question rewritten in its decoded, expanded form:
Silicon Valley has an enviable reputation as the home for hundreds of very successful high-tech companies. What were the conditions that made this possible? Now suppose that another country wanted to create their own Silicon Valley. What evidence suggests that this would be difficult? What evidence says that this would be easy? How credible or persuasive are these pieces of evidence? Finally, what do you think? Does the evidence lead you to conclude that Silicon Valley could be replicated or not?

Now that the task and the subject have been identified, is it possible to create a tentative outline that's tailored to this particular assignment question?
Yes, I think so:

- Introduction
- Supply some background on the history of Silicon Valley and, more importantly, list the characteristics that have made it such a successful part of the world

Worked examples

- Present the argument that agrees with the statement in the title; i.e. that Silicon Valley's special status is the result of factors that are very hard to replicate in other parts of the world
- Present the argument that disagrees with the statement in the title; i.e. the factors behind Silicon Valley's success can in fact be recreated anywhere else on the planet
- Compare the arguments and weigh up which evidence from each gives the most accurate picture
- Conclude with a personal judgement of how true/false the question's statement is

Alternatively, I could structure the essay like this:

- Introduction
- Supply some background on the history of Silicon Valley and, more importantly, list the characteristics that have made it such a successful part of the world
- Focus on one of those characteristics and assess how easy or difficult it would be to replicate it in a different location.
- Focus on a second characteristic and assess how easy or difficult it would be to replicate it in a different location. (... and so on, until the list of characteristics has been exhausted)
- Bring all of those characteristics together to compare the contribution that each of them makes to the success of Silicon Valley with the ease with which they could be reproduced
- Conclusion, with a judgement on how easy it is to replicate Silicon Valley

When researching, I can treat every bullet point in this outline as a 'container' in need of material to fill it. This gives me a good idea of what information I'm looking for and where to put it when I find it. Time to do some preliminary reading...

What information am I hoping that preliminary reading will reveal?

I'm not too concerned about finding information that helps me to decode the title further than I already have. I don't think that there's much more to uncover. However, I still need to gain a broad overview of the subject and of its literature. And I need to get some indication of the options that are available for my tentative outline.

Perhaps I'll discover that Silicon Valley has unique qualities that can't be replicated. Or maybe I'll learn that those qualities can actually be found anywhere. But more likely, I'll find out that the truth is somewhere between those two. That's a good thing, because it means that rather than answering the question with a "100% agree" or "100% disagree" response, I'll be able to fashion a balanced argument that's somewhere in between. And this means I'll have the opportunity to present evidence, show my own analysis of that evidence, build a well-constructed argument based on that analysis and conclude the argument with my own judgement. Fantastic!

What did preliminary reading reveal?

Firstly, I was right about the title; preliminary research didn't reveal anything new about the assignment that couldn't be deduced from the question's wording.

Secondly, I found out that Silicon Valley has a number of defining characteristics which contribute to its success as a highly prosperous region:

- Prestigious universities doing hi-tech research
- Readily available venture capital
- A supply of highly technologically literate workers
- An existing collection of hi-tech companies
- An adaptive and entrepreneurial culture
- A laid-back and non-conformist culture

So that lists the ingredients that I will need to talk about in the second section of the essay, after the introduction.

Worked examples

Thirdly, there are dozens of other 'silicon' locations (specialist vocabulary: 'tech clusters') in other parts of the world, such as Silicon Alley in New York, U.S.A. and Silicon Fen in Cambridge, England. However, these other locations have had varying degrees of success in replicating how Silicon Valley works. Discovering why some have worked well while others have failed will be a very important part of my in-depth research and will supply much of the material for the middle of the essay where arguments will be presented that either agree or disagree with the opening statement.

Finally, my preliminary reading also reveals some books that I need to get hold of and read:

1. *Regional Advantage*, Annalee Saxenian
2. *Clusters of Creativity*, Rob Koepp
3. *Building High-Tech Clusters*, Timothy Bresnahan
4. *Cloning Silicon Valley*, David Rosenberg

So, what now?

Well, now I know what I'm supposed to compose—and I even have a provisional outline for my essay. Preliminary reading has supplied material (characteristics of Silicon Valley and the discovery of other 'silicon'-named tech clusters) that will fill out some sections of the outline. This will turn it from a vague plan of how the assignment might look, to a more accurate representation of the final essay.

Once I have obtained the specialised books listed, I can begin some in-depth research. This is where I'll...
- Look more deeply into the situation, discovering and noting down the kind of information, viewpoints and statistics that give me a more complete understanding of how Silicon Valley works
- Search for the kind of evidence that quantifies the success of Silicon Valley's ambitious clones, to help me evaluate the accuracy of the statement in the title

- Assess all of that material and think about how to use it to construct the for/against arguments that will be at the centre of my assignment
- Conduct a search for other sources of information, such as relevant articles published in academic journals and anthologies

Worked examples

Example Question 2
Title:
"Compare and contrast the ways in which the Soviet Union's European allies responded in the late 1980s to Mikhail Gorbachev's policy of relaxing Moscow's control and granting them greater autonomy. How long did these responses last?" (European History)

What's the task type?
It's a comparison task, so I'll be expecting to put two (or more) things side by side and work out how they are similar or different and why these similarities and differences are significant.

Anything else to notice about the task?
Not really. There's an extra question tacked onto the end, but it refines the existing task rather than adding more tasks to it, so I wouldn't class this as a combination title.

Is the task predictable or unpredictable?
Comparison questions are predictable, so I should be able to borrow an existing blank template that corresponds to this task and then modify it for this particular assignment:

- Introduction
- Outline subject 1
- Outline subject 2
- Discern the areas of common ground between these subjects
- Discern the areas of contrast between them
- Analyse these areas and assess their significance
- Conclusion, with your own judgement

What's the subject?
The different ways in which the Soviet Union's European allies responded to Gorbachev's relaxing of centralised control from Moscow.

Is there more than one aspect to this subject?
There's no shortage here. Each satellite country's response could be treated as a single aspect of the subject, so I imagine that this question will have a great many aspects—perhaps too many!

Is there anything else to notice about the subject?
There are no unfamiliar words that I'm supposed to trip over. But there is an extra question, an unsubtle hint about the direction in which the essay should go: "How long did these responses last?" Perhaps the extra question also alludes to a hidden agenda; I will have to wait and see.

The same question rewritten in its decoded, expanded form:
In the late 1980s, the president of the Soviet Union, Mikhail Gorbachev, changed Moscow's policy of centralised control over its eastern European allies and gave them greater autonomy. What was the relationship before the change? In what ways did Gorbachev alter this relationship and why? Put each of the countries' responses to the change side by side to see how they are similar or different. What's interesting about this? Is there a pattern? Also: How long did the responses of these countries last? (...whatever that means!)

Now that the task and the subject have been identified, is it possible to create a tentative outline that's tailored to this particular assignment question?
Yes, but without further information, it still looks unwieldy and generic:

- Introduction and some background information on how Gorbachev changed Moscow's relationship with its European allies
- Outline how country 'A' responded
- Outline how country 'B' responded
- Outline how country 'C' responded (...and so on)

Worked examples

- Discern the areas of common ground between these responses
- Discern the areas of contrast between them
- Analyse these areas and assess their significance
- Conclusion, with my own judgement

What information am I hoping that preliminary reading will reveal?

Naturally, I want to get the broad overview of the subject and its literature that preliminary reading usually supplies. But after looking at the outline above, I'm worried that I'll have to write about each Eastern European country's response individually—so I'm hoping to find some kind of pattern within the responses. Not only would that save the essay from turning into a dreary list of countries, but I think it would give me a chance to apply some analysis to any such pattern and reach a judgement of my own.

And lastly, I'm unsure about that extra question tacked onto the end of the title, so my preliminary research must also assist with some further title decoding.

What did preliminary reading reveal?

In 1989 the president of the USSR, Mikhail Gorbachev, resolved to loosen the ties that bound the Communist countries in Eastern Europe to the Soviet leadership in Moscow. But the heads of those Eastern Bloc nations responded to this policy in very different ways:

a) Hungary and Poland both staged free, multi-party elections, the result of which almost entirely eradicated the Communist party from government. Hungary also dismantled the barbed-wire fence (part of the Iron Curtain) on its border with Austria.

b) By contrast, the old-style, hardline Communist leaderships of East Germany, Romania and Czechoslovakia were alarmed by Gorbachev's reforms, and outraged by Poland and Hungary's response to them.

Worked examples

So from this information alone, I can see that my assignment won't have to examine each country's response on an individual basis. Instead, I can assemble them into groups according to whether they embraced the new policy or whether they rejected it. And that's great because it allows me lots of chances to compare and contrast the two kinds of reaction.

However, I was still concerned about the extra question added at the end of the title and to what it referred. It cryptically asks "How long did these responses last?" To me, this implied that the responses of the Eastern Bloc countries didn't last long—perhaps because Gorbachev reversed the policy—before matters reverted to business as usual.

But research reveals that this question alludes to something more interesting. In countries where the reaction to Gorbachev's policy was multi-party elections, that response still exists because those countries have remained democratic to this day. However, the response from those governments that rejected the reforms didn't last long... because the governments themselves didn't last long! This twist was impossible to predict from the question, so it seems that my preliminary research has stumbled upon something of a hidden agenda buried within the title.

And yet this unexpected discovery isn't bad news. Not only has my research provided a general overview of the subject and decrypted the second part of the title, but it has also shown me how I might structure the assignment. In fact, it's the hidden agenda that has given me the chance to inject some critical analysis into the assignment and present my own judgement.

Here's how: All of the Eastern Bloc countries ultimately rejected Communism—a fact which could have made life difficult when trying to write an assignment that compares and contrasts them. However, the *means* by which this change was achieved varied. Because some of these transitions from Communist rule were peaceful and some were violent, my critical analysis could compare how each leadership responded to Gorbachev's policy (positively or negatively) with how that leadership ended (peacefully or violently). And then my

Worked examples

conclusion might comment upon whether there was a link between each regime's response and the manner in which that regime ended.

And as a starting point for that, I also now have a list of book titles to investigate:

1. *Gorbachev's Gamble: Soviet Foreign Policy and the End of the Cold War*, Andrei Grachev
2. *Revolution 1989: The Fall of the Soviet Empire*, Victor Sebestyen
3. *Seven Years That Changed the World: Perestroika in Perspective*, Archie Brown
4. *1989: The Year that Changed the World*, Michael Meyer

(In-depth research will also involve looking at other sources, such as newspaper reports or academic journals.)

So, what now?
Well, now that I have so much extra information, the first thing I should do is rewrite that awkward outline:

- Introduction
- Background information on how Gorbachev changed Moscow's relationship with the Eastern Bloc countries
- Outline how Hungary and Poland responded
- Outline how East Germany, Czechoslovakia and Romania responded (both to Gorbachev's policy *and* to Hungary and Poland's reactions)
- Talk about the areas of contrast between those responses (e.g. replacement of ruling party with free elections, reform of ruling party or violent government crackdown)
- Analyse the consequences for each type of response (i.e. how did different responses lead to the same outcome?)
- Conclusion, with my own judgement

I mustn't forget that this outline is only a suggestion for how I *could* structure my assignment; I'll be more certain of whether I can support it with evidence once the in-depth stage of research is well underway. But in the meantime, this is still a compact and workable starting point. Each bullet point gives me guidance when I'm conducting in-depth research on the information I need to uncover, whereabouts it will fit in and the role it will play.

Looking ahead, the to-do list for my in-depth research phase will look something like this...

- Establish in detail how each of the Eastern Bloc countries responded to Gorbachev's reforms.
- Try to compose a quick list of every comparable/contrastable aspect of these nations' transition from single-party Communism to multi-party democracy (e.g. relationship history with the Soviet Union, whether the leadership was hardline and orthodox or more liberal and flexible, how the leadership responded to organised opposition, etc.). I'm going to have to find plenty to talk about, so I really need to dissect these revolutions into many facets that can be examined and discussed.
- Determine whether these Communist nations can be neatly divided into two groups according to their reaction to the reforms. If so, then the job of comparing and contrasting them will be very easy. If not, then the comparisons and contrasts will be more complex.

Worked examples

Example Question 3

Title:
"Discuss the emergence and influence of 'New Hollywood' in the U.S. movie industry during the 1960s and 1970s." (Media Studies)

What's the task type?
It's a discussion task. As well as the obvious command word at the beginning, the question is very open-ended and gives no indication of some final objective that the assignment must achieve.

Anything else to notice about the task?
No, this task is quite straightforward.

Is the task predictable or unpredictable?
Recognising this as a discussion task doesn't help me to predict the structure of the essay—so it's unpredictable.

What's the subject?
The emergence and influence of New Hollywood in the U.S. movie industry during the 1960s and 70s.

Is there more than one aspect to this subject?
Well, if New Hollywood was something that surfaced in the 1960s and 70s, there must have been an Old Hollywood which preceded it. So if I assume that 'before' and 'after' are the two aspects from which I view the arrival of New Hollywood, I'll have some context for the changes it brings.

Is there anything else to notice about the subject?
The most attention-grabbing element is the term 'New Hollywood'. Clearly, that's something that I'm supposed to focus on and investigate. But I mustn't ignore the reference to *two* stages in the development of New Hollywood: emergence and influence.

The same question rewritten in its decoded, expanded form:

(This is difficult to do with an unpredictable task and so little information to work with, but here goes...) What was Hollywood like up until the 1960s and how did it work? Why did 'New Hollywood' emerge in the 1960s? How was it different from Old Hollywood? How did it influence the U.S. movie industry?

Now that the task and the subject have been identified, is it possible to create a tentative outline that's tailored to this particular assignment question?

Because this is an unpredictable task, I can't just refer to a ready-made outline and use it as a starting point for my own work. Therefore, I'm forced to create my own outline from scratch. However, there are clues in the question's subject to help me to do this. Logically speaking, New Hollywood had to 'emerge' before it could 'influence', and this sequence will be reflected in the overall structure of my essay.

And the subject has one other inescapable characteristic: the *emergence* of New Hollywood won't be something to debate—it's just a matter of historical record. But the *influence* of New Hollywood is very much open to examination. This is where I spot an opportunity to turn the vagueness of an unpredictable task into something much more concrete: if I treat this assignment as a combination of tasks, I can *describe* the emergence of New Hollywood and then *evaluate* its influence. Fantastic! So there's not much to go on, but the best outline I currently have looks something like this:

- Introduction
- Depiction of Hollywood before New Hollywood
- Description of the emergence of New Hollywood and why it was different
- Evaluation of the degree to which New Hollywood influenced Old Hollywood

Worked examples

This feels like a little bit of solid ground, and I hope that matters will improve when I've carried out some preliminary research.

What information am I hoping that preliminary reading will reveal?

Preliminary research's first duty will be to finish my decoding of the title by explaining the term 'New Hollywood'. I imagine that this explanation will quickly broaden into a wide overview of the film industry in the 60s and 70s, together with a clarification of the difference between Old Hollywood and New Hollywood. I'll also be looking out for the titles of suitable books for my in-depth research.

Additionally, I need to remember that I've been given an unpredictable task which requires that I build my own essay structure. At the moment, the most promising arrangement looks to be the one that I laid out above: *describing* New Hollywood's emergence and then *evaluating* its influence.

However, there's a chance that preliminary research might uncover something that undermines this simple plan, and so I'd need to look for other areas of interesting debate. For instance, sources might discuss whether there was really anything new about New Hollywood or reveal an ongoing academic disagreement over how much influence New Hollywood had over the industry. These are just random examples; preliminary reading should expose the genuine opportunities to compose a thought-provoking assignment.

What did preliminary reading reveal?

It revealed a heck of a lot...

In the late 1950s and early 1960s, the big Hollywood studios were dominated by producers, directors and department heads who were in their sixties and seventies. Their films were made to a formula, in the belief that sticking to tried-and-tested recipes was a safe bet. Such movies were based upon well-worn storylines, populated by predictable stereotypes and usually finished with a happy ending.

But in the 1960s, this business model began to falter as television decimated the regular movie-going audience. In response, movie studios poured a great deal of money into the production of extravagant films—only for them to flop at the box office. The future of the big studios was in mortal danger.

Research suggested that the movies made by the aged studio bosses did not appeal to the tastes of the young people who made up the majority of the cinema-going audience. The post-war baby boomers who were coming of age in the 1960s rejected the safe and expensively produced musicals and historical epics that Hollywood offered. Instead, they preferred to see films featuring characters to whom they could relate and storylines that dealt with controversial issues or that made some thought-provoking social comment. These young people discovered that the foreign films shown in art-house cinemas offered an alternative to Hollywood's tired template, and these films became very popular.

But these foreign films didn't just have an impact on movie consumers. The storytelling and film-making techniques of European and Japanese cinema also influenced young American film-*makers*. Rather than allowing their film-making ambitions to be stalled by a lack of Hollywood-style funding or equipment, these budding cinematographers made the most of whatever limited resources and money were available and created movies which mimicked the techniques they'd seen foreign directors employ.

It was only a matter of time before Hollywood crossed paths with these maverick film-makers. In 1966, Arthur Penn and Warren Beatty teamed up as director and leading man to make *Bonnie and Clyde*. Beatty supplied some of the funding for the movie from his own pocket and convinced Warner Bros. to provide the rest. In the same year, *The Graduate* was being produced by the independent movie producer and distributor Embassy Pictures.

The controversial nature and new cinematographic techniques of these films was a far cry from the Doris Day romantic comedies that studios had been releasing at the time—

and also unlike those films, they didn't flop at the box office. In fact, they brought in tens of millions of dollars. Hollywood noticed, and the big studios became much more willing to finance the projects of young directors with radical ideas about what a film should look like.

This phase in the American movie industry's history, between 1967 and 1980, came to be known as 'New Hollywood', and it produced such films as *2001: A Space Odyssey*, *Rosemary's Baby*, *The Godfather*, *Dirty Harry*, *One Flew Over The Cuckoo's Nest*, *Butch Cassidy and The Sundance Kid*, *Apocalypse Now* and *Alien*.

Ironically, the success of New Hollywood sowed the seeds of its own demise. Upon the release of *Jaws* and *Star Wars*, both were box-office smash hits. This had three consequences.

Firstly, large corporations noticed how profitable the movie business could be and began to buy up the large studios. These corporations were more interested in commercial success than quirky storylines, and New Hollywood's experimental filmmakers were no longer needed. Secondly, Hollywood studios decided that they now understood how to create their own high-grossing movies. A new formula had been discovered, and 'blockbuster' became a new genre. Lastly, movie directors who'd had total control spent even bigger budgets. But the gamble went horribly wrong in the early 1980s when a couple of very expensive films—*Heaven's Gate* and *One From The Heart*—flopped massively. Thereafter, the studios become unwilling to cede such complete control. New Hollywood's era of original films made by maverick directors was over.

...Well, this is what preliminary research has revealed, and it's completed my understanding of the question. I now know that 'New Hollywood' describes a period between about 1967 and 1980 when Hollywood released movies which broke away from the well-worn formula that Old Hollywood had been using (and losing money on). New Hollywood's movies were director-driven rather than studio-driven, confronted controversial topics, often made a social or political statement, weren't afraid to feature anti-heroes rather than heroes and didn't always finish with a happy ending.

But crucially, this research has confirmed that I **can** use my initial, provisional outline, because...

- There's plenty of material that conveys how the Old Hollywood system worked—so that's something I'll be able to depict.
- I've uncovered reasons for the *emergence* of New Hollywood and a clear picture of what was new about it—which I can now confidently describe.
- The biggest relief is that there's a wide range of areas where I can evaluate the *influence* of New Hollywood on movie-making, such as the introduction of dark and provocative storylines, the degree of control given to the director, reduced filming budgets, cinematographic techniques that were borrowed from foreign films, increased freedom to experiment with new film-making methods, alternative funding methods and alternative distribution arrangements.

But what if my original idea for an outline *hadn't* been feasible? All would not have been lost, because my preliminary reading also turned up interesting or even contentious areas that would have provided some starting points for creating a 'Plan B' outline:

- The strong influence of world cinema on many leading figures in the New Hollywood movement makes me wonder whether New Hollywood really was new—or was it borrowed?
- I also wonder whether the independent producers who originally financed many young film-makers' projects back in the early 1960s aren't being given enough credit; was their funding the *real* reason that the New Hollywood movement could emerge and make an impact on the whole industry?
- Is it accurate to portray the young film-makers of the early 1960s as *deliberately* trying to change the way Hollywood

worked—or was the discovery of New Hollywood just a fortunate accident for Old Hollywood?
- Perhaps most intriguing is how the New Hollywood story ended: Old Hollywood took New Hollywood's methods and reduced them to a recipe that it could follow on its own. Was this New Hollywood's most enduring legacy?

But as things turned out, I probably won't need to pursue those angles.

Finally, the research also gave me a good overview of the timeline of major events that my assignment will be covering, and some book titles to get my in-depth research underway:

1. *Easy Riders, Raging Bulls*, Peter Biskind
2. *New Hollywood Cinema: An Introduction*, Geoff King
3. *Scenes From a Revolution: The Birth of the New Hollywood*, Mark Harris

Looking back at the section where I listed what I *hoped* preliminary reading would reveal, it seems that everything on the checklist has been crossed off. Great!

So, what now?

Now that I have confidence in my original plan, I can revisit that tentative, provisional outline that I sketched before. Here are the first three bullet points…

- Introduction
- Depiction of Old Hollywood and how that worked
- Description of the emergence of New Hollywood and why it was different

But the last bullet point from that outline is:

- Evaluation of the degree to which New Hollywood influenced Old Hollywood

What this means is that I will have to examine both the characteristics of Old Hollywood that *were* radically changed by New Hollywood and those characteristics that remained largely unaffected. From this, I should start to get a feel for the kind of argument that I think I can make and support with evidence: Did the new school exert a great deal of influence on the old? Some? Or very little? Then I'll decide how best to present that case. But what help can I get with this?

Looking back at the section on evaluation tasks, there were two suggested structures for evaluation assignments. These structures represent either the "divide between what supports and what contests" approach...

- Provide the arguments and evidence that agree with the statement given or that adopt a particular position when answering the question
- Provide the arguments and evidence that disagree with the statement given or that adopt an alternative position in answer to the question
- Compare and evaluate the arguments that agree and disagree
- Conclusion (with your own judgement)

...or the "separate the subject into individual characteristics" approach...

- Discern one particular area relevant to the statement given (or question asked) and assess it from alternate perspectives (what do different viewpoints say about this aspect of the statement/question?)
- Discern a second area relevant to the statement given (or question asked) and assess it from alternate perspectives
- Discern a third area relevant to the statement given (or question asked) and assess it from alternate perspectives
- Compare and evaluate all perspectives that agree and disagree
- Conclusion (with your own judgement on the matter)

Again, it's the process of examining, analysing and criticising the evidence that will help me to pick the most suitable structure—or create one of my own.

This is great. I feel quite optimistic about this outline, because it delivers what I think my lecturer would want: a discussion which demonstrates that I've studied New Hollywood, how and why it came about and what effect it had. But I've also managed to turn an unpredictable discussion task from a potentially dreary and woolly monologue into a debate with conflicting views and a problem which I try to solve. I may yet make changes to this outline as I uncover further details, but it's a good starting point. The best news is that I know what I'm supposed to do and I have a good idea of how I'm going to do it.

So, the next job is in-depth research, which will include:

- Finding out more details about the way the big studio system worked in the days of Old Hollywood.
- Reading more thoroughly about New Hollywood. I'd like a more comprehensive list of the ways in which New Hollywood influenced Old Hollywood.
- And it would be nice to know the box office takings before and after this period to establish the degree to which New Hollywood financially affected cinema and studio revenues.

CHAPTER 9
AUTHOR'S NOTE

Well, that just about wraps up all of the advice that I can give you about essay title decoding.

Thank you for reading and I sincerely hope that from now on, whenever you're presented with one of those pesky essay questions, you'll be able to see straight through the cryptic jargon to the task and subject that are hiding behind it.

If you did find this book helpful and you'd like to spread the word, please consider leaving a review on the bookseller's website. If I can show more people how to decode titles, I might just reduce the stress levels of students everywhere.

Thanks again.

JRH.

Printed in Great Britain
by Amazon